_____

Rainy, Windy, Snowy, Sunny Days

WITHDRAWN

Literature Bridges to Science Series

The World of Water: Linking Fiction to Nonfiction. By Phyllis J. Perry. 1995.

The World's Regions and Weather: Linking Fiction to Nonfiction. By Phyllis J. Perry. 1996.

Rainy, Windy, Snowy, Sunny Days: Linking Fiction to Nonfiction. By Phyllis J. Perry. 1996.

Rainy, Windy, Snowy, Sunny Days

Linking Fiction to Nonfiction

Phyllis J. Perry

TEACHER IDEAS PRESS
A Division of
Libraries Unlimited, Inc.
Englewood, Colorado
1996

TEACHER IDEAS PRESS
A Division of
Libraries Unlimited, Inc.
P.O. Box 6633
Englewood, CO 80155-6633
1-800-237-6124

Production Editor: Jason Cook
Copy Editor: Curtis Holmes
Typesetting and Interior Design: Kay Minnis

Library of Congress Cataloging-in-Publication Data

Perry, Phyllis Jean.
    Rainy, windy, snowy, sunny days : linking fiction to nonfiction :
grades K–5 / Phyllis J. Perry.
    xviii, 147 p. 22x28 cm.
    Includes bibliographical references (p. 137) and index.
    ISBN 1-56308-392-2
    1. Children's literature--Study and teaching (Elementary)
2. Fiction--Study and teaching (Elementary) 3. Prose literature--
Study and teaching (Elementary) 4. Weather in literature--Study
and teaching (Elementary) I. Title.
LB1575.P47   1996
372.64'044--dc20   96-3751
                                                    CIP

For
Casey, *Clare*, and *Julia*,
who brighten every one of my days.

Contents

**Part II
Windy Days**

Part III
Snowy Days

Part III
Snowy Days
(*continued*)

Part IV
Sunny Days

Part IV
Sunny Days
(continued)

■ **NONFICTION CONNECTIONS** (continued)

Part V
Additional Resources

About the Series

In the era of literature-based reading programs, students are involved in narrative texts more than ever, but they still face difficulty when confronted with expository text. Many experts believe that one of the best ways to teach a subject is to *engage* the learner, that is, to get the student interested enough in a topic that the motivation to learn increases.

The Literature Bridges to Science series seeks to use the power of fictional works to bring students from the world of imagination to the world of fact. In this series, fiction is used to build interest, increase familiarity with a topic, enlarge background knowledge, and introduce vocabulary. The fiction is intended to be enjoyed, letting the power of the story create a desire to learn more about a topic. Several fictional works are used, which suit both individual tastes and the breadth of experience in a group of students.

As student interest builds naturally, one or more "bridge" titles are used to pique interest in a topical exploration. At this point, the teacher can introduce a main theme of study to the class, being confident that the learners are not starting at ground zero in their background knowledge of that topic. Interest in the topic might then be high enough to motivate students to attack the expository writing in works of nonfiction.

Just as several fictional works are used to introduce a topic, the Literature Bridges to Science series suggests that numerous nonfiction works be offered to students as they begin their topical explorations. The series is particularly useful to teachers who are transforming their teaching style to a cross-curricular content approach. Nonfiction titles are chosen carefully to represent the more literary treatments of a topic in contrast to a textbook-like stream of facts.

Introduction

This book is designed to assist any busy elementary teacher who is planning an integrated unit of study involving weather and seasons of the year. It includes suggestions for individual, small-, and large-group activities across the disciplines. The range of titles allows for student choice based on interest and skill level. The titles were selected from a large number of books recommended by children's librarians.

Between the fiction and nonfiction books in each section are two books that are suggested to serve as "bridges." These bridges combine factual information and fictional elements. This blend of fact and fiction enables the reader to make an easy transition from one type of material to another.

Parts I, II, III, and IV begin with summaries of fiction books, with discussion starters and suggested multidisciplinary activities following each summary. Next are summaries of related nonfiction books of various lengths and levels of difficulty, with suggested topics for further student investigation following each summary. The suggested activities involve skills in research, oral and written language, science, math, geography, and the arts.

Each part begins with a "bookweb" suggesting ideas for discussion and projects that might come out of the fiction, bridge, and nonfiction materials. All of the suggested books were published since 1980 and are readily available. They represent many cultures and include folk tales and legends.

📖 Teaching Methods 📖

One Teacher with Multiple Teaching Responsibilities

In most cases at the elementary level, a single teacher is responsible for teaching a variety of subject areas to a group of students. If the same teacher is responsible for teaching language arts, social studies, math, and science, the multidisciplinary approach suggested here will have a unifying effect on the curricula.

Before beginning a unit on weather, for example, the teacher might present one of the fiction books as a read-aloud in class. This helps set the tone for the upcoming unit of study. As they hear a good piece of literature dealing with some aspect of the weather, students begin to learn vocabulary, and to focus on rainy, windy, snowy, and sunny days.

The teacher might suggest that students be alert to information about weather. Students might be encouraged to bring articles clipped from newspapers and magazines to create a classroom vertical file. If a television special is scheduled that focuses on some aspect of the weather, or on some region, such as the rain forests, the teacher or another student could alert the class to the opportunity for viewing.

When the unit of study begins, the teacher might have each student select one of the fiction titles in part I and encourage small-group discussions among those who have read the same book. This extends reading skills, listening skills, and the use of oral language.

For the bridge books, the teacher might want to work with the class as a whole, assisting students who do not feel as comfortable with nonfiction as with fiction. Because the bridge books combine elements of a story or real-life adventure with information and facts, students are assisted in the transition from the one type of reading to the other. Their growing vocabulary and knowledge about the world of weather from the works of fiction will be assets for reading, understanding, and appreciating nonfiction.

As a composition activity, the teacher might assign writing topics concerning weather and then combine these with a science assignment. In this way, a student studying hurricanes, for example, will do library research and, where appropriate, prepare a bibliography and write an informative paper.

As a creative-writing assignment, the teacher might have each student write an original work from the point of view of a kite caught in a rainstorm. This would be an excellent time to use poetry related to weather and seasons. A collection of poetry is included in each of the major weather parts in this book. Students may read poems and experiment with writing their own.

The teacher might also select books that combine social studies and geography as students learn about Chico Mendes and the Amazon rain forest or Tepui's day in the rain forest along the banks of the Orinoco River.

Departmentalization with Team Planning

In schools where there is departmentalization but team planning time, the language arts, social studies, and science teachers might plan a unit on seasons and weather. The science teacher might concentrate on setting up a weather station and helping students increase their understanding of thermometers, barometers, rain gauges, and weather maps. The social studies teacher might use the unit to discuss tropical rain forests and to concentrate on map reading, making maps and using legends, computing distances on maps, and so on. The language arts teacher might create reading, research, and writing assignments that center around both the fiction and nonfiction books in the unit. Panel discussions and oral presentations of material will further speaking and listening skills. Specific skills such as skimming, reading for information, note taking, outlining, and using an index or a glossary of terms, might also be introduced or reinforced using the suggested nonfiction books.

Some students will find it easy to process information presented in the nonfiction books as pictures or as graphs and charts. For other students, these may be new sources of information. The math teacher might explain how to "read" these special materials, and might create assignments that involve students in constructing charts and graphs.

Specialist teachers might also be involved in this unit. The music teacher might incorporate songs of the seasons. The art teacher might use mobiles, tropical fish tissue paper collage, clay models of rain forest creatures, and so on during this period. Classroom and hall bulletin boards might feature a season of hurricanes and typhoons or an environmental project in some rain forest.

If a computer lab is available, software dealing with weather and seasons might be highlighted. Students might also use the computer stations and word-processing software to compose their written reports related to this unit of study.

If the media specialist is the one responsible for teaching research skills to students, this teacher might focus on using a CD-ROM encyclopedia that features hurricanes and typhoons, a vertical file on plants of the rain forest, or a computer-database search for topics related to the Arctic. The media specialist might highlight those magazines and books in the collection that deal with seasons and weather, and might even do some interlibrary loans to increase the materials available during this unit.

Team Teaching

In those schools where team teaching occurs, team members might choose to present their favorite lessons and experiments. Choices might be based on personal expertise or interest in a new topic. Next, teachers might map out a sequence and timeline for their students that shows the connections between subject areas.

While one teacher is presenting a lesson, colleagues might assist by leading small-group discussions, providing assistance with science experiments, or supervising small-group or individual research in the media center.

Some activities in a team teaching situation can be presented to a large group of students. Showing films or videos falls into this category. Team members might then designate stations or break-out groups where smaller numbers of students have the opportunity to extend their knowledge.

📖 Culminating Activities 📖

Whatever the configuration of students and teachers, there might well be an opportunity for a special culminating activity for each part of this unit of study.

For example, part I deals with rainy days. The teacher might confront students with a hypothetical scenario: they live in an area where severe flooding occurs. If this happened along the banks of the Missouri or Mississippi River, would students lose everything? Or is it likely that the president would declare this region a disaster area? Have one group of students research past floods in the United States to find out whether or not the floods were designated as disasters, and to find out about the cost and time involved in cleanup of the flooded areas. Have another group research a famous hurricane disaster in Florida or Texas to find out whether or not it was designated as a disaster, and to find out about the cost and time involved in the cleanup. Then, have the two groups debate whether it is more dangerous to live along a river that floods or in a coastal area that is hit by hurricanes.

As an example for a culminating activity for part III, have students plan the budget and all the arrangements for an imaginary trip to a famous ski resort. How much would round-trip airfare cost for the class? What would it cost to charter a bus, and what route would be followed? What lodging is available at what rates? How much should be allowed per day for the cost of food, lift tickets, and entertainment? Have students create a trip itinerary that involves them in both mathematics and geography skills.

Different culminating activities will come to mind as students become immersed in their reading. Students might want to forecast the future. Will the time come where acid rain and global warming make great differences in the production of food and in population centers in the United States?

📖 Scope and Sequence 📖

Part I covers rainy days. The fiction books include picture books, chapter books, and books about the rain forests. Each book deals with some aspect of rain. The nonfiction books are also related to rain, clouds, acid rain, flooding, and tropical rain forests.

Part II deals with windy days. The fiction books include picture books and chapter books. The nonfiction books are related to wind power, destruction from hurricanes and tornadoes, hot-air ballooning, flight, and weather prediction.

Part III concerns snowy days. The fiction books include picture books and chapter books. The nonfiction books provide information to help students understand snow, avalanches, glaciers, ice ages, snow sports, and life in the Arctic and Antarctic regions.

Part IV involves sunny days. The fiction books include picture books and chapter books. The nonfiction books deal with topics such as sunshine, summer activities, solar power, heat, radiation, and droughts.

Part V is a list of additional resources. There are listings of other fiction and nonfiction books for each of the four major parts: rainy days, windy days, snowy days, and sunny days.

Part I
Rainy Days

Rainy Days

● **FICTION** ●

📖 *Anna's Rain*
📖 *Enora and the Black Crane: An Aboriginal Story*
📖 *The Great Flood Mystery*
📖 *The Great Kapok Tree, A Tale of the Amazon Rain Forest*
📖 *Listen to the Rain*
📖 *Rain Talk*

📖 *Rainflowers*
📖 *The Rains Are Coming*
📖 *Small Cloud*
📖 *We Hate Rain*
📖 *Weather Report: Poems Selected by Jane Yolen*
📖 *Where the Forest Meets the Sea*

◆ **BRIDGES** ◆

📖 *Chico Mendes, Fight for the Forest*
📖 *One Day in the Tropical Rain Forest*

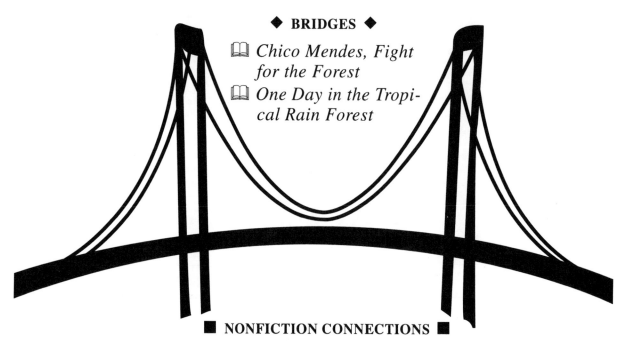

■ **NONFICTION CONNECTIONS** ■

📖 *Acid Rain*
📖 *The Acid Rain Hazard*
📖 *Antonio's Rain Forest*
📖 *Experiments That Explore Acid Rain*
📖 *Flash, Crash, Rumble, and Roll*
📖 *Jungles and Forests*

📖 *Rain*
📖 *The Rain Forest*
📖 *Rain Shadow*
📖 *Spring Weather*
📖 *Tropical Rainforest*
📖 *Why Are the Rain Forests Vanishing?*

—**OTHER TOPICS TO EXPLORE**—

—Acid rain	—Clear-cutting	—Clouds	—Dams
—Experiments with water	—Hydroelectric power	—Jungle plants	—Lightning
—Rain forests	—Rain shadows	—Thunder	—Weather forecasting

● *Fiction* ●

📖 *Anna's Rain*

📖 *Enora and the Black Crane: An Aboriginal Story*

📖 *The Great Flood Mystery*

📖 *The Great Kapok Tree, A Tale of the Amazon Rain Forest*

📖 *Listen to the Rain*

📖 *Rain Talk*

📖 *Rainflowers*

📖 *The Rains Are Coming*

📖 *Small Cloud*

📖 *We Hate Rain*

📖 *Weather Report: Poems Selected by Jane Yolen*

📖 *Where the Forest Meets the Sea*

 *Anna's Rain*

FICTION

by Fred Burstein
Illustrated by Harvey Stevenson
New York: Orchard Books, 1990. 32p. (unnumbered)

This very simple story would be appreciated by primary-grade students, as a silent read or as a read-aloud. The text is minimal, embodied in only one or two sentences on each page. The soft, realistic illustrations are done in muted tones and most often occupy a two-page spread.

As the story opens, Anna Lee is climbing onto a flower pot—to be tall enough to reach inside the big chest on the porch and fill a mug with bird seed. Although she spills some, she tells her father not to worry, because she is sure the raccoon will clean it up that night.

Even though it is raining, Anna Lee, wearing her coat and boots, insists on feeding the birds. Father tells her that birds do not eat when it is raining, but Anna Lee believes that they are cold, and that they might starve.

Father offers an umbrella, but Anna Lee has a better idea. She will ride on her father's back. So out into the cold rain they go—Anna Lee holding the mug of bird seed and her father giving protection to his rider by holding the umbrella above her. They put the seed into the feeder and then Anna Lee urges her father to run home because it is so cold.

Back inside their warm house, they watch and see many different kinds of birds immediately come to the feeder. Two jays seem to be talking. Father imagines that one is saying, "Snow tonight," while the other says, "Thank you, Anna."

Discussion Starters and Multidisciplinary Activities

1   Birds usually do not come out in the rain. They fluff their feathers and take shelter in nests and trees. Ask students why the birds in this story immediately flew down to the feeder as soon as Anna Lee had filled it.

2   There are no words on the last page of the book, but the action is unmistakable. Have students write a closing sentence for this page. Ask students whether they like the story better with or without the final sentence.

3   When Anna Lee said to her father, "I'm not doing anything," she really was doing something. Ask students what Anna Lee was doing and why she answered her father as she did.

4   Anna Lee and her father thought that the chirping birds sounded as if they were carrying on a conversation. Have students write original short stories that feature the song or call of a bird.

5   Have students look closely at the illustrations of the bird feeders—they contain sunflower seeds and millet. Have a few students research this topic. What kinds of birds eat what kinds of seeds? Are the beaks of birds that eat millet different from the beaks of birds that eat sunflower seeds? Have students share this information with the class.

6   On pages 28 and 29 of the book, the illustrations show seven birds at the bird feeder. The prose notes that two are jays. Have interested students identify the other birds at the feeder and then share this information with the class.

📖 *Enora and the Black Crane: An Aboriginal Story*

FICTION

by Arone Raymond Meeks
New York: Scholastic, 1991. 32p. (unnumbered)

The author tells a legend of when the world was new, a legend of the Kokoimudji tribe of Australia. Every other page of this large-format book is a full-page illustration. Although the text is simple, this format will appeal to elementary students interested in legends and original art.

The tale concerns Enora, a young man living in a rain forest. There are delicious fruits, rivers full of fish, and flocks of black, white, and grey birds flying above.

As the story begins, Enora is swimming in the river with his friends. He sees a flash of color among the trees and follows it. Enora comes to a clearing where there are many birds. The colors flow over the birds, and their feathers begin to glow with color.

Enora stays so late that when he gets back to camp, his family is worried and angry. No one listens to his story. That night he dreams that he is flying. Early the next morning, Enora returns to the clearing, hides in a tree, and watches. He sees the birds and kills a crane to take back to prove what he has seen.

But when the crane dies, it loses its colors. His family is sad that he has killed a bird. Feathers begin to grow out of Enora's hand. That night he dreams again of flying. The next day, he is covered in small black feathers. He returns to the clearing. Colors flow over the birds, but Enora's feathers remain black.

Discussion Starters and Multidisciplinary Activities

1 This legend recounts how many of the birds in the rain forest got their beautiful colors. Have students discuss Enora's killing of a crane to bring back proof of what he had seen. Was his punishment (being turned into a black crane) appropriate? Would students miss having birds with beautiful, colored feathers?

2 Because Enora dreams of flying, have students discuss whether or not Enora was happy as a crane.

3 Meeks makes paint from clay and berries, and paintbrushes using his own hair. Ask your art teacher or other resource person to discuss Aboriginal art with your students. Are there other famous Aboriginal artists?

4 Many people dream of flying. Have a small group of interested students research this topic. Who were the pioneers of manned flight in airplanes and balloons? When and where did this early exploration take place? Have students share what they learn with the class.

5 The first time the birds of the rain forest gather in the clearing there are cassowaries, scrub hens, parrots, and lyrebirds. Have a small committee of students find pictures of these birds to share with the class.

6 Meeks grew up in Australia near Dunk Island. He studied art at the Queensland Institute of Technology and at the City Art Institute in Sydney. Have students locate these places on a map posted on a classroom bulletin board.

 **The Great Flood Mystery**

FICTION

by Jane Louise Curry

New York: Atheneum, 1985. 171p.

This book will appeal to fourth- and fifth-grade readers.

The story begins with three sixth-graders, Gordy, Zizzy, and Roy, who are active children with superactive imaginations. They describe seeing lights in the Battaglia's house while the owners are away. The police find no intruder, and this reinforces Gordy's father's opinion that the children cannot be believed.

Gordy's family rent out their house for the summer because his father is out of work and needs money. They go to live with Aunt Willi and help her with some carpentry work. While there, Gordy searches for a hidden room and also researches old records about homes that were built there before the great Johnstown, Pennsylvania flood of 1889.

Aunt Willi's 107-year-old friend, Mr. Wegener, who was a draftsman in an architectural firm, helps Gordy.

The children are suspicious of the ponytailed man they keep seeing and of Professor Schuman who has rented Gordy's house for the summer and is also researching the time of the flood of 1889.

After several false starts, the children solve the mystery and discover the strongbox that survived the flood. The box contains a few valuables, but they had hoped for a big treasure. Still, everyone is cheerful. Gordy's dad will take courses and has a new job. The family will stay with Aunt Willi for a while. The board game the children are working on is nearly complete, and more adventure seems to be waiting just ahead.

Discussion Starters and Multidisciplinary Activities

1. Ask students whether they would rather have Gordy, Zizzy, or Roy for a best friend. Have students explain why.

2. Aunt Willi and Mr. Wegener are old, but they are mentally active and alert. Did it surprise the readers that someone over 100 years old could play such a major role in helping the children solve a mystery?

3. Ask students: If you had fallen into a hole beneath the house as Gordy did, and hurt yourself, do you think that you would have continued to look for the strongbox? Would you have started yelling for help when you heard your family's voices above you?

4. The building plans in this book are interesting. Ask a local architect to visit your class and bring the blueprints for a house or another building. Have the architect explain the drawings and how they are made and used.

5. Professor Schuman disguised himself well. If there is a local theater group in your city or town, invite an actor or actress who specializes in makeup to come to your classroom. Ask the actor or actress to use makeup, wigs, beards, and so on to demonstrate how people can radically change their appearance for a stage role.

6. Have interested students research the Johnstown flood of 1889. What caused the flood? How many people were killed? What damage occurred? Have students share what they learn.

FICTION

📖 *The Great Kapok Tree, A Tale of the Amazon Rain Forest*

by Lynne Cherry

San Diego, CA: Harcourt Brace Jovanovich, 1990. 36p. (unnumbered)

This large-format book with simple text and large, color illustrations will appeal to primary-grade readers.

The book tells the story of a community of animals living in a great kapok tree in the Amazon rain forest. As the tale begins, two men enter the forest. One points to a tree and then leaves. The other, using an ax, begins to hack at the tree. The wood is hard, and the man grows tired and sits at the foot of the tree to rest.

While he sleeps, animals of the rain forest come and whisper in his ear, warning him not to cut down the tree and telling him why he should not do so. Each offers a different reason why the kapok tree should be spared. The first animal is a boa constrictor. The snake is followed by a bee, a troupe of monkeys, a toucan, a tree frog, a jaguar, four tree porcupines, an anteater, a three-toed sloth, and a child from the Yanomami tribe.

When the man awakes, he sees the child and all the silent rain forest creatures around him. He also becomes aware of the sun streaming through the canopy, and of the plants and flowers hanging from the kapok tree.

The man picks up his ax to begin chopping at the tree again. Then he hesitates and looks at the beautiful scene around him. He drops his ax and walks out of the rain forest.

Discussion Starters and Multidisciplinary Activities

1   Each animal offers a reason for sparing the great kapok tree. Ask students which animal was most persuasive and why?

2   When the Yanomami child whispers to the sleeping man, he says, "When you awake, please look upon us with new eyes." Ask students what the child meant by this?

3   The man in this story reflects on the beauty and richness of the rain forest and decides not to cut down the great kapok tree. When the tale ends, the man is walking out of the forest. Have students discuss what might have happened next. Did the man simply leave and find another kind of job? Did the man persuade others not to cut down the trees? Was another man sent to do the tree cutting?

4   Have students choose one of the rain forest animals shown in the border of the world map at the front of the book. Have each student make a shoe-box diorama showing the animal's natural habitat, including a small likeness of the animal. The animals could be made from paper or could be small plastic or stuffed toys.

5   A sloth is a very slow creature. Have students write an original story in which a sloth's slowness plays a major role.

6   There are many unusual butterflies in the rain forest. Invite a guest speaker who can bring a butterfly collection to share with the class.

 # Listen to the Rain

FICTION

by Bill Martin Jr. and John Archambault
Illustrated by James Endicott
New York: Henry Holt, 1988. 32p. (unnumbered)

Primary-grade readers will enjoy this book. The text is minimal but manages to catch the rhythm and sound of rain. The full-page color pictures are muted in tone, combining realism and abstraction.

The book opens with the command to listen to the rain. A seashell is pictured on the beach. Students who have listened to the sounds of the sea by holding a shell to their ear will understand the mood of "catching" sounds. The next page uses rhyme to capture the feel of the first drip-drops—the first "wet whispers" of the coming rain.

As more drops are illustrated, the text explains how the rain begins to sing. Pitter-patters and splish, splash, and splatters are the sounds of the rain hitting the sea. A long-horned grasshopper, also a music maker, is shown beneath a branch as the rain sings.

As the rain begins to roar and pour, seeds from a dandelion are knocked loose and fly away. Waves form on the sea in a hurly-burly, topsy-turvy way beneath the lashing and gnashing teeth of the rain. Lightning flashes, thunder crashes, and the rain pounds down.

After the rain, there is a mishy, mushy, muddy puddle and a drip-drop that finally ends in silence. The final illustration shows a brilliant rainbow in the aftermath of the rain.

Discussion Starters and Multidisciplinary Activities

1   The illustrations in this book are exceptional. Have students tell the class which illustration was their favorite and why.

2   The rain makes a lot of other sounds not mentioned in this book (spattering against window panes, gushing down the rain spout, etc.). Have students close their eyes and imagine that it is raining. Then have students tell whether they were inside or outside, what sounds they heard, and what sights they saw.

3   Students may notice that people are missing from this book. Have students discuss why the author and illustrator included no people in their story.

4   Invite students to make "word squares" using words from the book. In this example, the teacher writes the word *rain* and then students complete the square. There are many possible answers.

```
R A I N
A     O
I     S
L A N E
```

5   Ask students to write or dictate an original short story. You are a kite flying high. It starts to rain. What happens to you?

6   Although it may rain hard, the number of inches of rain from a storm is usually minimal. Bring a large coffee can to class. On a rainy day, set it outside the classroom in a safe place where it will not be disturbed. Wait 24 hours, or until it stops raining. Bring the can inside and measure the amount of rainfall using a ruler marked to the 16th of an inch. How much rain fell?

 *Rain Talk*

FICTION

by Mary Serfozo

Illustrated by Keiko Narahashi

New York: M. K. McElderry Books, 1990. 24p. (unnumbered)

Primary-grade readers will enjoy this story, told in the first person by a little girl. There are soft, watercolor illustrations of this black child and her family.

One rainy summer day, a little girl and her dog play outside and listen to the sounds of the rain. The text is onomatopoeic; that is, it tries to capture in words the actual sounds that the rain makes. The first raindrops go *ploomp*. These are the first big drops that fall in the soft summer dust on a country road.

On the old tin roof of the garden shed, the raindrops all talk at once and say, "*Ping Ping PinaDing, Ping Ping Ping Ping Ping*." The water gushing out the drainpipe seems to *chuckle*. When it hits the pond it makes a *PlipPlipPlip* sound.

On the highway, as cars and trucks drive though the water, the raindrops bounce and *whoosh* and *hiss*. As they fall against an umbrella, the rain says *Bup Bup*. On the windowpanes of the house, rain sounds like pebbles and makes a *Flicking* sound. The raindrops that fall down the chimney *Spit* and *Sizzle* on the logs.

The little girl in this story gets tired after her busy day in the rain. She is tucked into bed, listening to the rain going *Drum-a-tum* on the roof above her.

The next morning when the little girl awakens, the rain is gone. There is a wet sparkle caught on some spider webs and flowers, and she looks for a rainbow.

Discussion Starters and Multidisciplinary Activities

1 Sometimes the little girl in this story is pictured wearing rain boots and sometimes going barefoot. Ask students to notice at what point in the story she takes off her boots. Have them discuss why she takes off her boots.

2 None of the characters in this story has a name. Discuss why the author did not give a name to anyone in the story. Have students choose a name for the little girl and for her dog. Why did they select these names?

3 Have students write an original story in which a rainbow plays a part. Have students share their stories with the class.

4 The rain in this story makes many different sounds. Glasses filled with varying amounts of water also make different tones when struck with a spoon. Have children experiment with different amounts of water in numbered glasses and then write and play a tune for the class.

5 Working with an adult volunteer or a media specialist, have a small group of students research rainbows and share what they learn with the class. What are all the colors in the rainbow? In what order do they appear? What causes a rainbow in the sky? Have students try to create a rainbow using a prism, a piece of white paper, and sunlight.

6 Bring to class data showing the monthly rainfall for your city or town. Have students construct a bar graph to show this data visually, labeling one axis with inches of rain and the other axis with months of the year.

 # *Rainflowers*

FICTION

by Ann Turner
Illustrated by Robert J. Blake
New York: HarperCollins, A Charlotte Zolotow Book, 1992. 32p. (unnumbered)

This picture book, suitable for primary-grade readers, describes a thunderstorm that sweeps across the field sending mice to their nests, woodchucks to their holes, and foxes to the shelter of the woods. Then, suddenly, everything grows still and the birds and animals emerge.

The book's first two-page spread is without text and simply shows a soft, color drawing of lightning bolts flashing across a dark sky above fields and a farm. After the opening, each two-page spread contains about five to twenty words.

The next two pages show a child, running from the field toward the house, carrying a pumpkin. The mice are pictured hurrying to hide in grass nests, and the next pictures show a wet woodchuck lumbering to its hole. The following scenes show grasses, trees, and flowers bending in the wind and rain.

Lightning bolts flash in the sky above the cornfield. This sends the sheep, horses, and foxes running while the geese ride out the storm in the reeds at the edge of the pond.

The sun bursts through the clouds above the barn, and the child catches drops of rain that roll off the roof. The chipmunks scurry back, and the woodchuck sticks up his head. The horses dance, and the trees are filled with robins that look like flowers among the branches.

Discussion Starters and Multidisciplinary Activities

1 From the text and pictures, have students guess what season of the year it is and offer support for their opinion. (They will probably select late summer or autumn because of the cornstalks and the pumpkins in the pictures.)

2 Ask students if they have ever been in a thunderstorm. Where were they? Was it exciting or frightening? (Students can share their experiences and feelings.)

3 Mice are favorite storybook characters. Ask students if they have ever read or heard a story that featured a mouse. What story was it? Was the mouse in the other story a field mouse that lived on a farm, or did it have different adventures?

4 The name of this book is *Rainflowers*. Discuss how the book got this name. Ask students to draw their own pictures to illustrate the last page of the book.

5 The woodchuck shown on the book's cover, as well as inside, is an interesting little animal. Have a small group of interested students research the woodchuck with the help of an adult volunteer or a media specialist. How big is a woodchuck? Where do they live? Are they called by any other name? What do they eat? Have the group share their findings with the class.

6 The sound of thunder is easy to recognize. Other sounds are not as easily identified. Ask a pair of students to record sounds around the school. Play the recordings and see if other students can guess what made each of the sounds.

📖 *The Rains Are Coming*

FICTION

by Sanna Stanley
New York: Greenwillow Books, 1993. 24p. (unnumbered)

This story, suitable for primary-grade readers, is set in the lower western area of the Republic of Zaire, a large country in central Africa. It is slightly below the equator. French is the official language of the country, but another language, Kikongo, is also spoken.

The softly colored illustrations provide an interesting look into the life of people in Zaire. They show a great variety of daily activities and indicate the kinds of clothing, housing, and animals common in the village.

A young girl, Aimee, who has been with her parents in Zaire for four months, tells the story. During that time, it has been very dry. Aimee's missionary father is training people to be pastors and teachers.

As the story begins, it is almost time for Aimee's party. While waiting for her father to come home, Aimee runs through the village, inviting her friends to come to the party. Each friend is busy with something, but promises to come soon. The phrase repeated throughout is in Kikongo, "Zimvula zeti Kwiza," which the author translates as "the rains are coming."

Father and the children arrive just in time to help Aimee and her mother move everything inside the house for the party, just before it begins to rain.

Discussion Starters and Multidisciplinary Activities

1. Help students locate Zaire on the map. Also indicate the line on the map that shows the equator. Discuss with students that there are two major seasons in this area: a rainy season when it is hot, and a dry season when it is coldest.

2. Have students study the pictures and then discuss what kinds of clothes are worn in Zaire in the dry and coldest season. What might the temperature be?

3. Have students study the pictures. What might the people in this village eat? (The pictures show a fish trap, the pounding of manioc into flour, and chickens, pigs, goats, and baskets of fruits.)

4. Ask students if they can think of something that a child in Zaire does that they do not, and something that a child in Zaire does that they do, too. (Possible answers might include: Carrying a basket on one's head is common in Zaire but not here. Going barefoot and attending parties are common events in both Zaire and here.)

5. One of Aimee's friends was pounding manioc into flour. With the help of an adult volunteer or a media specialist, have a small group of interested students research manioc and share what they learn with the class. (Manioc is a white, potato-like root that is peeled, soaked in water, and dried in the sun.)

6. Siamu and her father were mending a fish trap. How does this kind of trap work? Have an interested student research this and share what he or she learns with the class?

📖 *Small Cloud*

FICTION

by Ariane

Illustrated by Annie Gusman

New York: E. P. Dutton, 1984. 24p. (unnumbered)

This Native-American tale will be enjoyed by primary-grade students. The color illustrations are simple and stylized.

The story begins with a description of Small Cloud's mother, Singing River, and father, Big Sun. As Singing River dances in the warmth of the sun, a mist slowly rises above the river. One drop at a time, Small Cloud is born.

When Small Cloud is grown, she wants to go over the mountain. Her mother waits for her while Whistling Wind helps Small Cloud across the mountain, and Big Sun watches over her.

Whistling Wind blows Small Cloud across one mountain and shows her corn growing in the valley. Then he blows her over another mountain to a desert. He urges her to hurry. Beyond the desert, Small Cloud finds a lake where there are other little clouds to play with.

Then all the little clouds are blown into another valley where rain is needed. Small Cloud and her friends join together into a great cloud and begin to fall as rain.

After the corn receives the rain, the drops slowly return to Singing River, and the process begins anew.

Discussion Starters and Multidisciplinary Activities

1 There are several small animals pictured in this book. Have students look for these and try to identify them.

2 Singing River asks Big Sun to watch over their child. Have students study the pictures in the book to see if Big Sun carries out his responsibility.

3 Have students look carefully at the drawings of Singing River and notice how the illustrator connected her with water. (Her hair is like river water. She is dressed in green and blue. She wears a shell around her neck. Her skirt has fish on it.)

4 The story of *Small Cloud* is often depicted as "the water cycle." Using one of the nonfiction books that shows the water cycle, have a student draw the water cycle on the chalkboard. Then ask another child to tell the story of *Small Cloud* pointing out where each part of the water cycle appears in the story.

5 In an acrostic poem, the first letter of each line spells the name of the poem. Have students write a poem about one of the characters from this story. For example:

B eaming down on Singing River
I nhabiting the sky
G lad to see dancing.

S miling at the world,
U nder a cloud
N ever neglecting his family.

6 Have a small group of students work with a media specialist to draw, label, and bring to class four or five pictures of different clouds. Have each student show the class what kinds of weather are associated with that particular cloud.

 *We Hate Rain*

by James Stevenson
New York: Greenwillow Books, 1988. 32p. (unnumbered)

FICTION

Second- and third-grade readers will appreciate this book, written and illustrated in a cartoon-like format. It is a tall tale in which Grandpa tells Mary Ann and Louis about a rain that occurred when he and his brother were young. Color pictures show the characters' comments in balloons above their heads. A simple text appears at the bottom of each page.

Mary Ann, Louis, and their dog, arrive at Grandpa's door saying that they hate rain and have not had any fun for days. Grandpa invites them in and tells them about the rain that fell when he and his brother Wainey were young. Grandpa tells them that it rained for weeks until the water came up to the porch, and the boys had to stay indoors.

Then the water came into the house and reached as high as their beds.

The pictures show Grandpa and his brother in a house filled with several feet of water. They practice the piano, ride a tricycle, dive off the furniture, sail boats, and blow soap bubbles. Friends float in and out the windows. Strange fish visit, and the family finally moves up to the roof.

When the rain stops, the house is full of water, so Grandpa dives into the water, swims down to the bathroom, and pulls the bathtub plug so the house dries out.

Grandpa's story ends as the rain stops. He, his brother, and the children go outside to enjoy sunshine and ice cream.

Discussion Starters and Multidisciplinary Activities

1 This story is a tall tale in which everything is exaggerated. Have students study the pictures and point out several things that happen in the story that could not happen in real life.

2 Grandpa's mother planned to divide a cookie into five pieces and give a piece to everyone in her home. Ask students: If you were going to divide cookies in half, how many cookies would you need to give everyone in your class one-half of a cookie? How many cookies would be needed to give everyone one-third of a cookie?

3 Grandpa's brother was called "Wainey." Ask students what name they would give Grandpa. Why?

4 When they ran out of food and were perched for the night on the roof of their house, each member of Grandpa's family had a dream. Grandpa was hungry and dreamed of strawberry ice cream. Have students make pictures of the favorite food they might dream about. Share these with the class.

5 Some strange fish swam into Grandpa's house. Have students write poems about some of the strange creatures that might have swum into Grandpa's house when it was filled with water. Illustrate and post these on a bulletin board.

6 As a class project, begin to tell a tall tale. The teacher begins, naming a few characters and giving the setting. The teacher stops after an exciting twist in the plot, and then a student adds to the story. Continue until each student has had a chance to add to the tale. You might record the tale and allow those who are interested to listen to the tale again.

From Rainy, Windy, Snowy, Sunny Days. © 1996. Teacher Ideas Press. (800) 237-6124.

Weather Report:
Poems Selected by Jane Yolen

Illustrated by Annie Gusman
Honesdale, PA: Boyds Mills Press, 1993. 64p.

FICTION

In this book, well-known author Jane Yolen has selected more than 50 poems. The book is divided into five sections: One Misty Moisty Morning: Rain; Rays in the Middle of the Great Green Sea: Sun; I Will Blow You Out: Wind; Icicle Popsicles: Snow; and On Little Cat Feet: Fog. This book is decorated with a few black-and-white drawings.

This book might also be used with part II, "Windy Days"; part III, "Snowy Days"; or part IV, "Sunny Days." Poems related to rainy days include those by Beverly McLoughland, H. W. Longfellow, John Ciardi, Langston Hughes, Christine Crow, Jane Yolen, Ralph Fletcher, Mark Van Dorn, Anna Kirwan-Vogel, Maud E.Uschold, and Anna Grossnickle Hines, as well as a selection from Mother Goose and a Hopi prayer.

The poems are different in mood, structure, use of rhyme and meter, and focus. Some students will enjoy listening and picking out the various sounds of thunder and rain in the poems. Some will enjoy the nonsense poem, "Rain," while others will like the details included in "Frogs and Rain." The regular rhyme and rhythm of "November Rain" will appeal to some readers, while others will enjoy the condensed image, made without the use of rhyme, created in "Just When I Thought."

Discussion Starters and Multidisciplinary Activities

1. Read to your students "Chatterbox, the Rain" and "April Rain Song." The poets concentrate on the sounds made by falling rain. (In one, the rain is like a chatterbox that will not stop talking. In the other, the rain is like a lullaby.) Ask students what sounds they hear when they listen to the rain. Is it more like a chatterbox or a lullaby? Which poem do they enjoy most and why?

2. Read to your students "Rain in Summer" and "November Rain." Ask students what impressions of rain they get from these poems. Each poem creates a very different mood. What is the mood of "Rain in Summer?" What is the mood of "November Rain?"

3. Some people like rain, while others hate it. Ask students to express their feelings about the rain.

4. "A Writing Kind of Day" suggests that words are like rain that hit the page. Ask students to read and think about the poem and then write their original poem which describes how they view the act of writing.

5. Have each student make up a riddle or a tongue twister about rain and share it with the class.

6. Have students create a board game with markers that move down a path through a rain forest. Prepare a deck of cards with math problems. If a student turns up a math card and gives the right answer, he or she rolls a pair of dice and moves the number of spaces shown. If "doubles" are thrown, it is "raining"—the player must move back to the first square.

Where the Forest Meets the Sea

FICTION

by Jeannie Baker
New York: Greenwillow Books, 1987. 32p. (unnumbered)

Most books about the rain forest feature the Brazilian Amazon rain forest. This book is set in the Daintree Wilderness of Australia and deals with the 296,000 acres of wet tropical rain forest wilderness in North Queensland. The text is simple, with only one or two sentences on each page. The beautiful, color illustrations reflect what the illustrator calls "collage constructions."

The story is told in the first person by a young boy who goes with his father in a boat, through the reef, to a part of the forest that has been there for more than 100 million years. This book creates an interesting mood. Drawings from the past and future are superimposed in faint outline on drawings of the present.

As the young boy walks and plays in the forest, he watches and listens. He is aware of the thick trees and vines and wonders about aboriginal forest children who may have played in the same place where he now stands.

The boy leaves the forest, walking toward the sound of the sea, and returns to his father who is cooking a fish. The boy likes the fish but feels sad because the day has gone so quickly. His father reassures the boy, saying they will come again, but the boy wonders if the untouched forest will still be there when they return.

Discussion Starters and Multidisciplinary Activities

1   As you show the collage illustrations to students, ask them to look for the parts of the drawings that are meant to show what lived there millions of years ago. When they find one of these parts, ask them to explain what the artist has done to make this portion of the drawing look "unreal."

2   We are not told anything about the rest of the boy's family. We only see him and his father. Ask students to do some imagining. Where do you think these two live? What is the father's occupation?

3   Ask students if they have been alone in a wooded area. What did they think about and imagine? Was it peaceful or scary?

4   The author of this book prepared the pictures as collages using lots of different materials including modeling clay, paper, textured cloth, natural material, and paint. Using the textured collage illustrations in this book as a springboard, have students create a collage of the Australian rain forest. Display the finished work.

5   The boy in this story imagined what it might have been like long ago. Have a group of interested students research what the place where they live might have been like long ago. Was it once under an ancient sea? Did other peoples live here? Was it a forest? A local historical library might be of help on this project.

6   Have a group of interested students prepare a large map of Australia for display, marking the Daintree Wilderness, major cities, and other tourist attractions.

◆ *Bridges* ◆

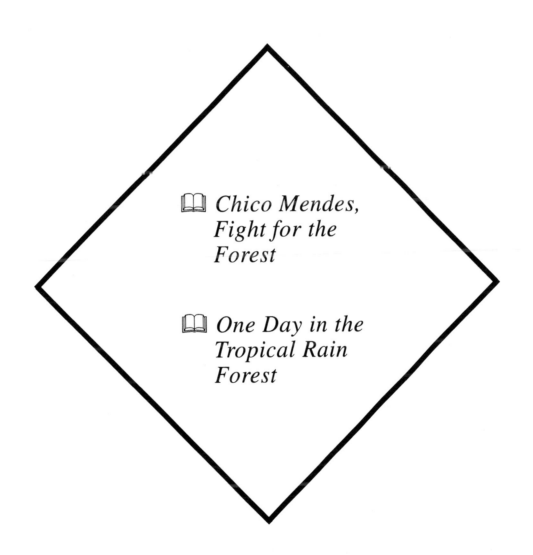

📖 *Chico Mendes,
Fight for the
Forest*

📖 *One Day in the
Tropical Rain
Forest*

 *Chico Mendes, Fight for the Forest*

BRIDGES

by Susan DeStefano
Illustrated by Larry Raymond
Frederick, MD: Twenty-First Century Books, 1992. 76p.

This book is mostly text, illustrated with a few black-and-white sketches. It is appropriate for readers in grades three through five. It is part of the Earth Keepers Series, which includes biographies of naturalists and environmentalists.

In chapter 1, Chico Mendes and a group of his followers are marching into the rain forest in the summer of 1986 to stage a peaceful protest against cutting down the trees. The chapter conclusion tells the reader that Chico Mendes was killed in December 1988.

Chapter 2 describes the Amazon rain forest, which contains more than 2.4 million square miles, 50,000 species of plants, and 3,000 kinds of fish. It describes how the rain forest ecosystem affects the entire planet.

Chapters 3 and 4 tell the history of rubber tappers and the lives that they lead. This section explains how the early Native Americans lived, how they used the forest, and how they came to work for estate bosses. The Native Americans received almost no money for their hard work. This section also describes how rubber tappers carry out their jobs.

Chapter 5 details the destruction of the rain forest. The National Integration Program began moving many people from crowded cities to the rain forests to farm.

Chapters 6 and 7 tell of the ways people have united to try to save the rain forest and how the struggle continues.

Possible Topics for Further Student Investigation

1. Although the destruction of the world's rain forests may seem like a simple, black-and-white issue to students, it is actually very complicated. Culture, modernization, supply and demand, economics, politics, and so on all play roles. Ask three students to make a case for cutting trees and clearing land for farming, and another three students to present the arguments against deforestation. Have students share their information in a debate format before the class.

2. Chico Mendes was a union leader. There have been many powerful labor union leaders in the United States. Have a group of interested students research labor unions in the twentieth century in the United States. Who were the important leaders? What is the AFL and the CIO? Have each student in the group prepare a short paper and photocopy a picture of a particular union leader. Display this information on a bulletin board.

3. Have a group of students use the information in this book to prepare a series of math problems to be solved by the class. For example, the Amazon rain forest includes 2.4 million square miles. Find the size of several of the smaller United States. How many of these states must be added together to equal the size of the Amazon rain forest? Another problem might ask how many electric-blue butterflies with eight-inch wings could rest, wing-tip to wing-tip, on the seven-foot-wide water lilies that live in the rain forest?

📖 *One Day in the Tropical Rain Forest*

by Jean Craighead George
Illustrated by Gary Allen
New York: Thomas Y. Crowell, 1990. 56p.

This book will appeal to intermediate-grade readers. It is mostly text, written as time notations or diary entries throughout a day. It contains a few black-and-white sketches.

Tepui is a young Indian boy who lives in a tropical rain forest in Venezuela. He loves his home and especially the capuchin monkeys, three-toed sloths, jaguars, scarlet macaws, and other wildlife that surround him.

When the story begins, it is early morning and Tepui hurries to join a group of five scientists who are studying the rain forest. Tepui knows that bulldozers and trucks are moving toward the rain forest today to cut down everything and ready the land for crops.

Tepui has helped each of the scientists find interesting specimens, but he has been unable to find a nameless butterfly. If he could find one, a wealthy industrialist would name it for his daughter and buy the tropical rain forest of the Macaw.

As Tepui and Dr. Rivero make one more hunt for a nameless butterfly, the creatures of the forest go about their daily routines. It rains in spurts, which slows the bulldozers.

Tepui leads the way to a tall tree, which he and Dr. Rivero climb. There they find and capture a nameless butterfly. Dr. Rivero rushes to call Caracas and saves the rain forest. Tepui hurries to tell the bulldozers that they can go home.

Possible Topics for Further Student Investigation

1. Page 3 of the book mentions the enormous Hercules beetles. Have an interested student research the beetles. Have the student find or draw a picture of a Hercules beetle and share this and other information about the beetle (such as size, food, and habits) with the class.

2. A great drama is going on throughout the book that could make a fascinating mural. One way to make the mural would be to put up a large sheet of background paper. At one spot, perhaps near the middle of the paper, have students draw the Coco de Mono tree and the nameless butterfly. Other students can select something from the book, make it using construction paper, and add it to the mural. Each student should label their addition. Students could choose: the jaguar and cubs, army ants, vines, moss, ferns, bromeliads, lizards, snakes, leaf-cutting ants, wasps, beetles, opossums, anteaters, tapirs, toucans, macaws, boa constrictors, marsupial mouse, tayra, agoutis, sloth, Hercules beetles, and so on.

3. This tropical rain forest is a very noisy place. There are bird calls, insect rattles and chirps, drops of rain falling, the rumble of the approaching trucks and bulldozers. Would there be a way to create and imitate some of these sounds? Have an group of interested students experiment with a tape recorder. Have them try to create these interesting sounds and then share their tape, and an explanation, with the class.

From *Rainy, Windy, Snowy, Sunny Days.* © 1996. Teacher Ideas Press. (800) 237-6124.

 *Nonfiction Connections*

📖 *Acid Rain*

📖 *The Acid Rain Hazard*

📖 *Antonio's Rain Forest*

📖 *Experiments That Explore Acid Rain*

📖 *Flash, Crash, Rumble, and Roll*

📖 *Jungles and Forests*

📖 *Rain*

📖 *The Rain Forest*

📖 *Rain Shadow*

📖 *Spring Weather*

📖 *Tropical Rainforest*

📖 *Why Are the Rain Forests Vanishing?*

Acid Rain

by Tony Hare

New York: Gloucester Press, 1990. 32p.

This is part of the Save Our Earth series of books, which seeks to increase the awareness of young students about environmental issues. This large-format book is illustrated with color photographs, drawings, and charts and is suitable for readers in grades three through five.

The book begins by introducing the importance of rain to life and the threat of air pollution, which is poisoning our rain. Pollutants include fuels burned in cars, homes, factories, and power stations, which combine with moisture in the air to form acids that fall to the ground with the rain.

Acid rain can be dangerous to humans; can destroy life in ponds, lakes, and rivers; can kill trees and plants; and can even damage buildings. Acid rain is not always wet; it sometimes falls as a dry dust.

Acid rain is a global problem. A world map on page 12 indicates actual and potential pollution spots. Not only does acid rain damage trees, soil, lakes, and rivers, but also ancient buildings and statues.

Smog in cities can irritate the lungs and eyes of the people who live there, and ozone pollution can damage the leaves of plants. The book concludes with a discussion of what can be done to reduce acid rain and pollution.

Possible Topics for Further Student Investigation

1. Interested students could create a class bulletin board depicting the food chain of a lake. Insects, small fish, larger fish, and water birds should be included. If there is a lake in a park near you, the students could contact the appropriate parks and recreation department and direct any questions they may have to a knowledgeable person on the staff. In addition to identifying captions, information could be included to indicate that if acid rain builds up in the water of a lake, the food web could be disturbed. Plants would die, the small fish that feed on the plants would have no food, and so on.

2. This book discusses how many trees in the Black Forest of West Germany have been destroyed by acid rain. Have interested students research this topic and share what they learn with the class. What sorts of trees once grew in the Black Forest? Where is the Black Forest located? What do scientists think is the source of the acid rain that is falling on the trees? What has happened to the trees that grow there? Is this problem continuing today?

3. Many cities and states have clean air laws. Some of these laws relate to if and when homeowners can burn wood in their fireplaces. Some laws relate to factories and industries in the area and any smokestacks that they may have, and other laws relate to fuels sold for cars and trucks. Have a pair of students investigate what sorts of clean air laws are in effect in your city and state. If possible, have the students bring in copies of laws and ordinances to share.

📖 *The Acid Rain Hazard*

by Judith Woodburn
Milwaukee: Gareth Stevens, 1992. 32p.

Third- through fifth-grade readers will enjoy this book, which is approximately half text and half color photographs and drawings. This book is part of a series called Environment Alert!, which introduces young readers to global problems facing our planet and to the interdependence of living things.

The book's first section, "Trouble from the Sky," explains what acid rain is, how it began, and where it occurs. Detailed examples include the Adirondacks, a land of dead lakes in the state of New York; and the disappearing Black Forest in Germany.

The second section, "Stopping Acid Rain," discusses how countries might reduce pollution from coal burning and how emissions from cars and trucks might be reduced. Two examples are cars with catalytic converters and the use of unleaded fuel. Machines called scrubbers, which are costly to install, can clean smoke before it comes out of factory smokestacks. Alternative power sources, such as using water and wind, are being explored.

The final section describes the debate over which methods and funding should be used to reduce acid rain. There are suggested research activities, and a list of things to do and places to write for more information. There is also a brief bibliography and a glossary of terms.

Possible Topics for Further Student Investigation

1 In some parts of the world, such as Palm Springs, California, there are thousands of windmills in wind "farms." These windmills each have three-blade propellers that rotate swiftly in the wind and power generators that produce electricity. Power like this, which does not rely on burning coal, can help reduce pollution. Have a group of interested students research wind farms. A media specialist might be able to help locate relevant magazine articles. Where are wind farms currently used? Are they effective? What are problems associated with them?

2 Have a group of students test a variety of common liquids using strips of pH-test paper and chart the results for classmates. Use a series of clean water glasses. Pour about one inch of each liquid to be tested into separate glasses. Dip an edge of the pH-test paper into the liquid and observe the color of the paper. Chart the results. Test liquids might include vinegar, lemon juice, orange juice, soda pop, tap water, milk, tea, and salt water.

3 Have a pair of interested students write for more information about acid rain. They should compose a short, clear letter explaining that they want this information to share with classmates. The letter writers should include a 9-by-12-inch, self-addressed envelope with postage attached to carry five ounces of mail. Send the letter to: National Clean Air Coalition, 530 7th Street S.E., Washington, DC 20003.

From *Rainy, Windy, Snowy, Sunny Days*. © 1996. Teacher Ideas Press. (800) 237-6124.

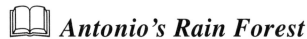

📖 *Antonio's Rain Forest*

Adapted from an original text by Anna Lewington
Photographs by Edward Parker
Minneapolis: Carolrhoda Books, 1993. 48p.

This is a real-life adventure illustrated by color photographs and drawings. It will appeal to third-, fourth-, and fifth-grade readers.

In chapter 1, the reader meets Antonio and his family, who live in western Brazil's Amazon rain forest. Antonio does not go to school because there are no schools in this part of the rain forest. He keeps busy helping his parents.

Antonio's father is a *seringueiro*, or rubber tapper, who collects white sap from wild rubber trees that grow along three paths near their home. The family use trees for building their houses and canoes, vines for brooms and baskets, and they eat fruits and hunt the animals of the forest.

In chapter 2, Antonio describes a forest trail where he often sees monkeys, birds, ants, lizards, and different kinds of trees.

Chapter 3 is about tapping trees, and chapter 4 explains how the latex is turned into rubber. Antonio's father cuts the tree and then places a tin cup beneath the cut; the cup fills with latex. Later, he collects the latex and turns it into rubber in a smoking hut. Or, the rubber is thickened by using ofe sap. Blocks of rubber are traded at the community warehouse.

The final chapter explains the problems involved in protecting tropical rain forests.

Possible Topics for Further Student Investigation

1   This book mentions an English chemist, Joseph Priestly, who experimented with sap from rubber trees that Europeans brought back after visiting Brazil in the 1700s. Have an interested pair of students research Joseph Priestly. Where and when did he live? What other discoveries did he make besides the eraser? Have students share what they learn with the class.

2   The tinamou bird sings at the same time every day. It acts like a kind of clock for the people who hear it. The thermometer cricket chirps in such a way that it serves as a thermometer for the people who hear it (by counting the number of chirps per minute, the listener can estimate the temperature). Have students research the thermometer cricket, make a sketch of it, and share what they learn with the class.

3   Three-fourths of all natural rubber is used to make tires. Natural rubber is stiff when it is cold and sticky when it gets hot. Vulcanization is a process of treating rubber that is of value to the mass production of tires. Have a small group of students research this topic. They should write a short paper explaining what vulcanization is and how rubber is treated and processed for manufacturing tires. At the end of the paper, students should list their sources of information, giving the name of the book or article, the author, and the date of publication.

Experiments That Explore Acid Rain

NONFICTION CONNECTIONS

by Martin J. Gutnik
Brookfield, CT: Millbrook Press, 1992. 72p.

Fourth- and fifth-grade readers will enjoy this book from The Investigate! Series. These books focus on important scientific issues, provide background information, and suggest interesting projects to increase understanding. The book contains a few black-and-white photographs and charts but is mostly text.

Chapter 1 provides an introduction to the topic of acid rain. Chapter 2 discusses nature's cycles. Chapter 3 explains what an acid is. Chapter 4 gives information on the formation and cause of acid rain. Chapter 5 deals with the effects of acid rain. Chapter 6 suggests what can be done about acid rain.

The processes of "scientific method" are explained and this format is used in the various projects outlined throughout the book. These include: an experiment with a green plant; a study of an ecosystem; identifying acids and bases; neutralizing acids with bases; studying the corrosiveness of acids; producing sulfur dioxide; making acid rain; monitoring acid rain; building an environment for acid rain experiments; studying the effects of acid rain on the pH of water and soil; and studying the effects of acid rain on aquatic and land vegetation.

The book concludes with a section on what can be done about acid rain.

Possible Topics for Further Student Investigation

1   One way for students to see the corrosive effect of acid on surfaces such as statues and buildings is to set up a two-week experiment. Purchase an unglazed bathroom tile from a tile or building supply store. Fill a clean medicine dropper with concentrated lemon juice. Drop some of the lemon juice onto the tile. Repeat this process every school day for two weeks. Always drop the lemon juice onto the same area on the tile. Observe what has happened after two weeks.

2   Students understand that in acid rain, the water droplets have picked up pollutants that fall to earth with rain. A pair of students might complete the following experiment to demonstrate how it rains: Pour a half cup of very hot water into a Pyrex jar. Cover the jar with a lid. Set a can of ice cubes on top of the lid. The hot water warms the air in the jar. The steamy air becomes water vapor. (If you shine a flashlight into the jar you will see a "rain cloud.") The warm air will cool when it comes in contact with the cold lid. It will condense back into water and drop like rain.

3   If your class is interested in learning more about acid rain, have one student write to: The Acid Rain Foundation, Inc., 1410 Varsity Drive, Raleigh, NC 27606 and ask that they send materials. Include a 9-by-12-inch envelope, self-addressed, with sufficient postage to carry four ounces of mail.

Flash, Crash, Rumble, and Roll

by Franklyn M. Branley
Illustrated by Barbara and Ed Emberley
New York: Thomas Y. Crowell, 1985. 32p.

Second- and third-graders will enjoy this book, which has simple text and amusing, color illustrations.

The book begins in a story-like format, showing a girl and her cat in a boat on a quiet, still day. There are clouds in the sky indicating that there may be a thunderstorm. The fluffy white clouds are shown turning grey and then black.

A diagram explains how warm air rises inside a cloud, carrying water vapor with it. When the water vapor cools, it changes into drops of water and crystals of ice. More charts and diagrams follow, indicating the movement of air inside a thunder cloud. Lightning and thunder are also explained in text and pictures.

In the story, rain begins to fall, gently at first, and then much harder, as part of a full-scale storm with wind, thunder, and lightning. The pictures show lightning striking high objects and rain flooding the gutters of the town.

The text gives safety tips to follow when there is a lightning storm: get out of the water, go inside the house, stay away from wires and metal, do not stand under a tree that is alone in a field, crouch down so you are not the highest thing around, stay inside a car.

The book concludes with the girl and her cat feeding the birds and watching a rainbow after the rain.

Possible Topics for Further Student Investigation

1. On a day when there is bright sunshine striking a window in the classroom, have an interested student make a rainbow indoors to show the class. First, fill a glass with water and stand it in a window in bright sunlight. Put a sheet of white paper on the floor below the glass. Position the glass and align the paper so that the sun shines through the water onto the paper. This positioning may take some time. When the objects are in the correct position, the light will refract like a rainbow onto the paper.

2. Have students make a variety of safety posters and hang them on the walls at school. You might first discuss various situations, including topics such as walking rather than running in the halls, using equipment on the playground carefully, and so on as possibilities for posters. Students might also want to include some weather-related safety tips. Pages 22 to 25 of *Flash, Crash, Rumble, and Roll* will provide good ideas. Remind students to include a brief caption as well as a drawing on their posters.

3. Often it seems to rain and spoil weekend fun. Read to students the poem "Rainy Rainy Saturday" by Jack Prelutsky. Have students discuss what they do when they stay indoors on a rainy day. Then provide students the opportunity to write their original rainy Saturday poems. These could be serious or funny, rhymed or unrhymed, illustrated or just text. Arrange the final products on a bulletin board.

📖 *Jungles and Forests*

by Clint Twist
New York: Gloucester Press, 1993. 32p.

Jungles and Forests is part of the Hands On Science Series that encourages young readers to enjoy science and connect it with their lives. This large-format book has color drawings and photos.

The book covers: forest zones, natural cover, tropical rain forests, diversity and how it works, temperate forests, species and soil, boreal forests, winter survival, other forests, forest management, and myths of the forest.

The book begins by pointing out that 10,000 years ago, the world's forests were twice as large as they are today. Human beings compete with forests for the land.

In this particular unit of study, the section on tropical rain forests is of greatest interest. The text explains that tropical forests grow well around the equator where temperatures usually range from 68 to 95 degrees Fahrenheit. This area also receives 80 inches of rain annually.

The largest of the tropical rain forests is in the South American Amazon river basin, but there is discussion of other rain forests including those of the West Indies and Africa.

This book describes each of the three layers in a tropical forest: the top canopy with a height of about 130 feet, a second canopy with a height of about 65 feet, and a third canopy with a height of about 33 feet. These layers have climbing plants and epiphytes growing in their branches.

Possible Topics for Further Student Investigation

1. One thing for which rain forests are famous is the diversity of butterflies that live there. Butterflies live in many parts of the world. Some are sure to live in your area. Put up a bulletin board display featuring butterflies. Include drawings and magazine pictures. Try to include pictures of butterflies that are found in the rain forest. Butterflies that you might want to include are: Zebra Swallowtail, Tiger Swallowtail, Mourning Cloak, and Painted Lady.

2. A rain forest with its canopy of trees, hanging vines, flowers, insects, and animals would make a great setting for a short story. Ask students to write original short stories set in the rain forest. Allow time for students to share their stories aloud.

3. Many students have planted seeds and watched them grow into plants, but students may not have tried to propagate plants in other ways. Set up an area in the classroom where students may try to propagate plants from leaves. They may want to do some initial research before beginning; for example, talking with someone in a local flower shop. Once plants have been selected, have students set the leaves of the plants in a clear plastic cup or glass in a sunny spot and observe them over a period of time. Eventually small roots will be seen and new leaves will begin to grow. When they are ready, move the sprouting leaves to the proper kind of soil and container and try to grow healthy new plants. African violets are one kind of plant that will propagate in this manner.

 *Rain*

by Joy Palmer

Austin, TX: Raintree Steck-Vaughn, 1993. 32p.

Second- through fourth-grade readers will enjoy *Rain*, a part of the First Starts series of books. *Rain* is illustrated with color drawings and photographs.

The topics presented in this book are: What Is Rain?; Water in the Air; Around and Around; Measuring and Forecasting; Thunderstorms; Rainbows; All About Raindrops; Plants Need Rain; Animals and Rain; Around the World; Living with Rain; Rain on the Ground; Using Rain; Acid Rain; and Things to Do.

This book helps develop a "weather vocabulary" by using and defining a few words in the glossary such as evaporation and condensation. There is a pictorial representation of the water cycle. There is also an explanation of how sunlight and rain make a rainbow.

There is a brief discussion of how plants need and acquire water, the needs of animals, and an explanation of rainfall variation. A photograph shows the wettest place on earth, Mount Waialeale in Hawaii.

This book presents methods of dealing with rain and water, including building homes on stilts in rainy areas to avoid flooding, and the use of gutters and drainpipes to carry rain off roofs.

The book concludes with a brief section on how rain is used by humans for drinking water and for growing crops, and the danger to our planet from the increase of acid rain.

Possible Topics for Further Student Investigation

1   Plants need water in order to live, but acid rain can kill plants and trees. You can simulate the effect of acid rain on plants. Purchase two small plants as close to identical in size as possible. Put the plants where they will receive the same amount of sunlight. Water each plant on the same schedule and give each plant the same amount of water. Label one plant "fresh water" and the other "lemon water." Fill two quart jars with tap water. Add two tablespoons of lemon juice to one jar. After a month, observe what has happened to the plant that received fresh water. What has happened to the one that received lemon water?

2   Some people say that they can tell when it is going to turn rainy and stormy because some part of their body aches. Could that be true? Can some people tell when it is going to rain? Ask the school nurse whether there is any truth in this. Or, have a child contact a doctor with this question and share the doctor's answer with the class.

3   A raindrop might fall anywhere. It could land on a lawn, an umbrella, a tropical rain forest, an ocean, a mountain top, a picnic table, a pony's back. Write an original story in which there is rain. It could be a nonfiction book tracing a single drop of rain through the water cycle. Or it could be a picture book in which the rainstorm has an effect upon the people or animals in the story. Allow enough time on another day so that students may share their stories with the class.

The Rain Forest

by Billy Goodman
New York: Tern Enterprise, 1991. 96p.

**NONFICTION
CONNECTIONS**

Third- through fifth-grade readers will enjoy this large-format book with approximately equal amounts of space devoted to text and to full-color photographs. The photographs are remarkable. It is divided into four major sections: "Inside the Rain Forest," "Animals of the Rain Forest," "People of the Rain Forest," and "Trouble in the Rain Forest."

"Inside the Rain Forest" describes the canopy or roof of the rain forest, which is made up of the crown of trees, the understory, and the plants that tolerate the shade in the lower portions of the forest. It is pointed out that a typical four-square-mile section of rain forest has approximately 1,500 species of flowering plants.

The section "Animals of the Rain Forest" explains that a patch of rain forest measuring four square miles typically has about 125 mammal species, 400 bird species, 100 reptile species, 60 amphibian species, and 150 kinds of butterflies.

The section "People of the Rain Forest" shows people who live today much as their ancestors did, securing food, building materials, and medicine all in the forest.

The concluding section, "Trouble in the Rain Forest," describes deforestation and the growing interest in extractive reserves where logging is prohibited and harvesting natural products is encouraged.

Possible Topics for Further Student Investigation

1 One of the interesting plants discussed in this book is the Strangler Fig. It is sometimes called *matapalo*, or tree killer. This plant begins its life in the canopy of a rain forest, drops roots to the ground, and strangles the host tree. With the help of a media specialist, have a pair of students research the Strangler Fig. In which rain forests does it grow? What happens after it kills the host tree? Does the tree bear fruit? Have students share their findings with the class.

2 Many creatures of the rain forest survive because of their camouflage. Ask an interested pair of students to study camouflage. They should check out books and magazines that have photographs demonstrating how difficult it is to spot a bird, insect, or reptile with good camouflage in its natural environment. Have students discuss camouflage and share their pictures with the class.

3 Page 94 of the book contains metric conversions that could be the source of interesting math problems. Using the information on this page, ask a small group of students to prepare some problems for the class to solve. One problem might be to convert the temperature 100 degrees Fahrenheit to Centigrade (subtract 32, multiply by 5, and divide by 9). Two other questions might be to calculate how many square kilometers are in 15 square miles? (15 x 2.5899) or to calculate how many pounds are in 113.3980 kilograms? (100 pounds = 45.3592 kilograms).

Rain Shadow

by James R. Newton
New York: Thomas Y. Crowell, 1983. 32p.

NONFICTION
CONNECTIONS

This is a simple text, appropriate for students in grades two through five, with lovely, soft pencil sketches. The book explores areas where geographical conditions are right to form a rain shadow. Rain shadows occur where there is a large body of water over which clouds form and winds blow the clouds inland. If these clouds reach a high mountain range that forces the moisture from them, there will be a lush growing area on one side of the mountain and an arid area on the other side.

In text and pictures, the differences between the two sides of the mountain are shown. For example, lush lodgepole pines may grow on one side of the mountain, and scraggly sagebrush on the other side.

Small line drawings are interspersed and labeled to identify different types of plants, water birds, and trees.

The clouds that reach the far side of the mountain lack moisture. As they pass over the area within the rain shadow, they drop only about 20 inches of rain a year. On the lush, ocean side of the mountain, however, there may be 200 inches of rain and snow.

Plants that live within the rain shadow, such as sagebrush, prickly pear, and bunchgrass, are adapted to live in the arid climate. The sagebrush is covered with hairs that trap and hold moisture. The prickly pear is covered in a waxy material and has spines instead of leaves. The bunchgrass may die off during long dry spells, and then grow from the roots after a rain.

Possible Topics for Further Student Investigation

1. By studying a map of the world, could students predict where rain shadows might exist? (They will be looking for areas with mountains close to the coast and where there are prevailing inland winds.) After students make predictions, have them research the average annual rainfall on both sides of the selected mountain ranges. Were the predictions correct? Were there some areas where there was no rain shadow?

2. One of the places mentioned in this book is the Patagonian Desert in South America. Locate this desert on a map. Have students research what kinds of plants and animals survive in these arid conditions and select one of the plants or animals of particular interest. Have students make a sketch and research interesting facts about the plant or animal chosen. Have students share this information as an oral report to the class.

3. There are many interesting Hawaiian names. They contain a lot of vowels. One name that is included in this book is the Ohia-lehua tree which grows on the island of Kauai. An interested student may make a salt and flour map of the Hawaiian Islands. It should be to scale in terms of the distance of one island from another and the relative size of each island. On the island of Kauai, ask the student to show a place where one might find an Ohia-lehua tree that is 100 feet tall and where one might find a 1-foot-tall Ohia-lehua tree. The student should share the map and explain the differences in full-grown tree growth.

Spring Weather

by John Mason

New York: Bookwright Press, 1991. 32p.

Third- through fifth-grade readers will enjoy this book from the Seasonal Weather series. The series describes and explains the types of weather associated with annual seasons and tells how weather affects the activities of people living in different parts of the world. The book is illustrated with color photographs and drawings. An index and a glossary are included.

Because spring is a changeable season, sharing some of the characteristics of winter and some of the characteristics of summer, spring may have both cold and warm days, windy days, and even days of late frost. The book is included here, however, because we associate rain showers with spring weather.

The teacher will also find *Spring Weather* useful to consult during the "Windy Days," "Snowy Days," and "Sunny Days" parts.

Sections include: "What Is Spring?" "The Earth and the Seasons"; "The Spring Season"; "The Earth's Atmosphere"; "The Wind"; "Clouds and the Water Cycle"; "Weather Systems and Fronts"; "Spring in Temperate Lands"; "Spring Around the World"; "Rainbows and Haloes"; "The Ozone Hole"; "Weather Forecasting"; and "Things to Do—Measuring Rainfall."

Because many students find that the best part of a rainy day is the rainbow that follows the storm, the section "Rainbows and Haloes" will be of special interest.

Possible Topics for Further Student Investigation

1 Daffodils and hyacinths are closely associated with spring. Three-dimensional hyacinths make an interesting art project. Have students cut a pair of leaves and a stem from green construction paper. Glue these onto a sheet of background paper. Cut one-inch-wide strips of pink and lavender crepe paper. Have each student choose a strip and cut the crepe paper into one-inch squares. Lightly draw the outline of the shape of the hyacinth blossom with a pencil. Starting at the stem, take a one-inch square of crepe paper and twist and hold it over a pencil eraser. Dip the paper into a small pool of glue. Press the eraser, covered in the crepe paper, onto the background sheet. Gently remove the pencil, leaving the bit of lavender or pink paper in place. Continue placing these "flowerets" close together until the outline of the blossom is filled.

2 Page 29 shows how to graph rainfall. Have students find the amount of rainfall in your area for each day of a spring month last year. Graph the data. For the same month this year, graph the data. Compare the two graphs.

3 Sometimes, after spring showers, there is a rainbow. Many beautiful stories have been written about rainbows. Ask students to write an original story about a rainbow. It can be fiction or nonfiction. Plan the text and pictures for a 32-page picture book. Students can write, type, or word process the text. When the books are finished, arrange for interested students to read them to a preschool or kindergarten class.

Tropical Rainforest

NONFICTION CONNECTIONS

by Michael Bright
Illustrated by James Macdonald
New York: Gloucester Press, 1991. 32p.

This book is part of a series, World About Us, which deals with the problems facing today's environment and suggests some possible solutions and alternatives. The emphasis is on making young people aware of action that must be taken to protect our world for future generations. This book is approximately one-half large-print text and one-half color drawings. It will appeal to primary-grade readers.

The book begins by explaining what a rain forest is and where the rain forests are located on earth. This is followed by an explanation of "the canopy," the "understory," and the "shade" of the rain forests. In a rain forest, there are a few very tall trees called emergents. Below them is a canopy of trees that gets most of the sunlight. Many birds and animals such as toucans, macaws, and monkeys live in the canopy. Small trees grow in the understory, and large animals, such as gorillas and leopards, live in the shade.

The book explains why rain forests are valuable and why they are currently in danger. Trees take in carbon dioxide and produce oxygen. The text explains that when trees are burned to clear the land, they release carbon dioxide into the air which can trap heat inside the atmosphere and cause global warming.

One section of the book is devoted to people of the rain forest and the riches found therein.

Possible Topics for Further Student Investigation

1 Camouflage is discussed in this book on page 10. Many insects, birds, and animals have special markings or colors that help them to match the color of their surroundings or confuse their enemies. Have a small group of students study camouflage. Have each member of the group choose a different moth, beetle, lizard, or bird with special markings. Have each student make a picture of the creature chosen and share it with the class, explaining how the camouflage works.

2 The lumber from trees in a rain forest is valuable. Ask a person from a local lumberyard to discuss with the class various kinds of woods, their differences, how they are used, and their comparative features and costs. If possible, small samples of different woods should be shared. Students might be responsible for inviting the guest speaker and for sending a follow-up letter thanking him or her.

3 Students might enjoy planning a special "Rain Forest Snack Time." Each student could volunteer to bring and share a product that originally came from the rain forest. Nuts, pineapples, oranges, bananas, and cocoa, are some possibilities. Along with a donation to the class snack, each child might write a sentence or two about the food shared. Does it still come from a rain forest or is it now raised somewhere else? With these sentences, the class could prepare a "menu" for the snack time giving the names of the foods and information about them.

Why Are the Rain Forests Vanishing?

NONFICTION CONNECTIONS

by Isaac Asimov
Milwaukee: Gareth Stevens, 1992. 24p.

This is a short, easy-to-read book that will be simple for primary-grade students to understand. The book is illustrated with large, color photographs and contains a glossary of terms.

This book begins by asking some questions about why people are currently chopping down vast areas of the tropical rain forests that have been standing for millions of years.

First, the author explains that rain forests exist in a green belt, known as the tropics, on either side of the equator. This is a wet area which gets as much as 200 inches of rain annually. This rain supports the tropical rain forests, including the high leafy canopy of trees, and the shady area beneath. Hundreds of species of trees may grow in such an area.

The rain forests also support hundreds of species of birds, millions of insects, and many unusual creatures, such as monkeys and panthers.

This book points out that in the past thirty years, more than half of the world's rain forests have been destroyed. Most have been cut down to create farmland. The soil is not rich, and when huge areas are cleared, the heavy rains wash away the thin layers of soil leaving barren land behind.

This book concludes by suggesting ways—using economic pressure—of preventing further clearing of the rain forests. Also included are addresses of places to write to obtain more detailed information.

Possible Topics for Further Student Investigation

1 Ask a small group of interested students to write to one of the addresses in the book (Rainforest Alliance and Greenpeace) and ask for additional information about rain forests. Students should include a large, self-addressed, stamped envelope. If students receive a reply, have them share the new information with the class.

2 The text points out that tropical areas may receive 200 inches of rain in a year. Have a small group of students do a rainfall graphing project. Have them pick out some cities in the United States and around the world and then research to find out their average annual rainfall. Have students prepare a large bar graph that lists the names of the cities along the horizontal axis and the number of inches of rain along the vertical axis. Have students share this information with the class.

3 After students have done considerable reading about the plants and animals that live in the rain forest, have each student prepare a riddle for classmates to solve. Have students find or draw a picture and write down several facts about the subject of the riddle. For example, a student might say, "I live in a tropical rain forest. I am a small animal that people eat for food. Some people say that I look like a long-legged guinea pig. What am I?" (Answer: an agouti.) After the riddle is solved, or after everyone gives up, have students share their pictures.

Part II

Windy Days

Windy Days

● FICTION ●

- 📖 *A Bed for the Wind*
- 📖 *Belinda's Hurricane*
- 📖 *The Blood-and-Thunder Adventure on Hurricane Peak*
- 📖 *Brother to the Wind*
- 📖 *Hurricane*
- 📖 *Hurricane City*

- 📖 *Jack and the Whoopee Wind*
- 📖 *Mirandy and Brother Wind*
- 📖 *The Turnaround Wind*
- 📖 *Voices on the Wind, Poems for All Seasons*
- 📖 *The Whirlys and the West Wind*
- 📖 *Wind*

◆ BRIDGES ◆

- 📖 *Catching the Wind*
- 📖 *Sailing with the Wind*

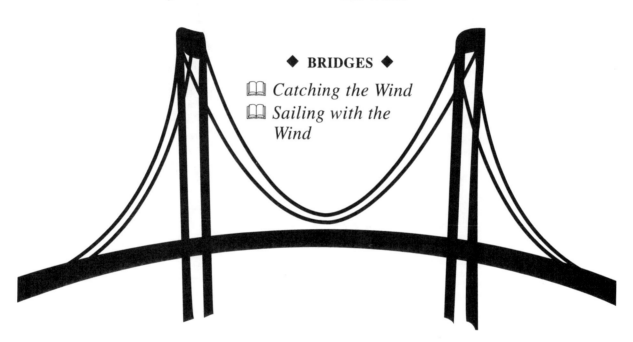

■ NONFICTION CONNECTIONS ■

- 📖 *The Air I Breathe*
- 📖 *Catch the Wind! All About Kites*
- 📖 *Changes in the Wind: Earth's Shifting Climate*
- 📖 *Facts on Water, Wind and Solar Power*
- 📖 *Flight*

- 📖 *Hot-Air Ballooning*
- 📖 *Projects with Flight*
- 📖 *Weather*
- 📖 *The Weather Sky*
- 📖 *Wind*
- 📖 *Wind & Water Power*
- 📖 *Wind Power*

—OTHER TOPICS TO EXPLORE—

—Beaufort scale	—Ballooning	—Climate	—Erosion
—Flight	—Hurricanes	—Kites	—Paper airplanes
—Tornadoes	—Typhoons	—Wind farms	—Windmills

From *Rainy, Windy, Snowy, Sunny Days*. © 1996. Teacher Ideas Press. (800) 237-6124.

Windy Days

● *Fiction* ●

- 📖 *A Bed for the Wind*
- 📖 *Belinda's Hurricane*
- 📖 *The Blood-and-Thunder Adventure on Hurricane Peak*
- 📖 *Brother to the Wind*
- 📖 *Hurricane*
- 📖 *Hurricane City*
- 📖 *Jack and the Whoopee Wind*
- 📖 *Mirandy and Brother Wind*
- 📖 *The Turnaround Wind*
- 📖 *Voices on the Wind, Poems for All Seasons*
- 📖 *The Whirlys and the West Wind*
- 📖 *Wind*

📖 *A Bed for the Wind*

FICTION

by Roger B. Goodman

Illustrated by Kimberly Bulcken Root

New York: Simon & Schuster, 1988. 32p. (unnumbered)

Primary-grade students will enjoy this picture book, which contains a fair amount of text. The full-color illustrations are especially intriguing.

This story is told from the viewpoint of a boy named Peter. As the story begins, Peter is getting ready for sleep. He is puzzled by the sad sound that the wind makes as it comes down the street. Peter asks his parents where the wind sleeps. His mother does not know. His father suggests that he should ask the wind.

Peter goes to the window and calls out when the wind comes from around the corner. The wind creates four small whorls of leaves and twigs on which to rest while talking to Peter. Peter asks the wind where it sleeps at night. The wind sadly tells Peter that it has not found a place to rest.

Peter volunteers to take his stuffed elephant and go with the wind to find a bed. First they go over the city, but the buildings are too sharp to make a good bed. Then the wind tries resting on top of a lake, but it is too wet and cold. A valley looks like a nice spot, but it is too small. Finally the wind comes to rest on a flat plain.

Peter gets sleepy too. When he awakes, Peter is at home in his own bed. He runs to the window to see, but there is no sound from the wind. Yet, in the light of the street lamp, he sees four small whorls of leaves and twigs.

Discussion Starters and Multidisciplinary Activities

1 Peter does not seem to be afraid of the wind. Ask students to look at pictures of the wind in this book. Does the wind look gentle or frightening? How does the wind act?

2 Many of these pictures include significant details. Ask students to study Peter's room and the picture of the ridge of rocky mountains. Let them take turns pointing out the different details that they find.

3 Peter had a lot of toys. Ask students why they think he took Jumbo the elephant with him on his adventure?

4 Ask students to write a legend explaining why the wind wanders about at night moaning and groaning and sounding unhappy. Have students share their completed legends.

5 This story could be a dream. Ask students to think about some of the pleasant dreams they have experienced. Then have them write a poem about a dream.

6 Students might want to make a board game based on this book. Markers could be small plastic elephants to represent Jumbo. The path of the board game would show a city, a lake, a valley, a plain, and Peter's room. A student rolls a die and moves the marker the number of spaces shown after correctly answering a question on the top card of a deck of cards. (These cards might be math facts, etc., with the correct answer shown on the back.) By landing on certain squares, a player might hit a sharp building or fall in the lake. Then the player goes back to "START." The first player to make it safely through the path, wins.

FICTION

📖 *Belinda's Hurricane*

by Elizabeth Winthrop
Illustrated by Wendy Watson
New York: E. P. Dutton, 1984. 54p.

Third- and fourth-grade readers will enjoy this short book, which has a few black-and-white sketches but is mostly text.

As the story begins, Belinda, visiting her Granny May, is sorting through shells. She hates the thought of going home after summer vacation. Belinda cuts her neighbor's lawn, avoiding the dog who does not like her. She has saved enough money to buy her grandmother a shell necklace for her birthday.

Belinda goes into town and learns that a storm is coming. She also discovers that someone else has bought the shell necklace from the shop. Belinda is determined to find out who made the necklace and to buy another one.

Granny invites Mr. Fletcher and his dog to ride out the hurricane in her house, where it is safer. The storm hits. To keep busy, Belinda starts to make a necklace for Granny May. Mr. Fletcher helps her. His dog is miserable, so Mr. Fletcher takes him outside, and the dog is swept away. Water is seeping into Granny's house. Granny, Belinda, and Mr. Fletcher move upstairs.

Belinda spies the dog and, tied to a rope, goes out to rescue it. Mr. Fletcher manages to pull them back inside the house. The storm ends. Mr. Fletcher gives Belinda another necklace for Granny May and makes plans to have her collect shells for him next summer.

Discussion Starters and Multidisciplinary Activities

1   Belinda says that Mr. Fletcher looks just like his dog, Fishface. Have students discuss what happens in the story and whether or not they think that these two look and act alike.

2   Some people love to visit their grandparents and others do not. Ask students why they think Belinda likes to visit Granny May. Belinda tells someone in town that one day she will come to the island and never leave. Ask if that is likely to happen.

3   When the story ends, Belinda and Mr. Fletcher have discussed being partners next summer. But Mr. Fletcher does not come out to see Belinda before she leaves or celebrate Granny May's birthday. Ask students if they think that is strange, or if it is in keeping with Mr. Fletcher's character.

4   Invite to the class someone who has a seashell collection. Ask the visitor to share some shells from the collection and explain what once lived in the shells and where they were collected.

5   Granny and Belinda both say "opposites attract" at some time during the story. Ask students to write an original poem about opposites.

6   Information is given about the Maine village where Granny May lives. Using the information from the book, have a small group of interested students make a map of the village. Show Granny's house, Mr. Fletcher's house, Mrs. Greenstone's house, Miss Lizzie's gift shop, the fishing docks, South Beach, the seawall, the grocery store, and Captain Jack's ferry.

The Blood-and-Thunder Adventure on Hurricane Peak

FICTION

by Margaret Mahy
Illustrated by Wendy Smith
New York: Margaret K. McElderry Books, 1989. 132p.

Third- through fifth-grade readers who have a whimsical sense of humor will enjoy this chapter book. Margaret Mahy has twice won the English Carnegie Medal. This story is told like an old-fashioned melodrama set in wonderland.

The Unexpected School sits on top of Hurricane Peak. Hurricanes rage every day and people venture outside only when the storm is on the other side of the mountain. Students wear stone boots so they will not blow away, as did their head mistress, Mrs. Thoroughgood. She has been gone for years, and Mr. Warlock takes her place and teaches the children magic instead of math.

Mr. Warlock has fled to the mountain from Belladonna Doppler, a beautiful and brilliant inventor. Warlock and Doppler love each other but have a conflict about magic and math.

The villains are: Sir Quincey Judd-Sprockett, an industrialist who wants to close the school and to marry Belladona; and his two assistants, Amadeus Shoddy and his son, Voltaire. Also featured prominently in the action are two cats, Zanzibar and Tango, and a number of students including Huxley Hammond and his sister, Zaza. Huxley likes to write bloodthirsty stories and his sister loves to illustrate them.

In typical melodramatic fashion, loves wins out, the school stays open, the villains reform (partially), and all ends well on Hurricane Peak.

Discussion Starters and Multidisciplinary Activities

1. Melodramas often have villains. Sir Quincey Judd-Sprockett is introduced as a wicked industrialist. Ask students to point out some of the ways in which Sir Quincey is and is not a typical villain.

2. Aunt Perdita is no other than Mrs. Thoroughgood. Ask students when they first started to suspect Aunt Perdita's true identity. What gave her away?

3. Voltaire mixes up parts of words when he speaks. Ask students whether they thought this added or detracted from the overall story. Was Voltaire's speech difficult to read and understand?

4. Have two interested students write an original conversation that might have taken place between Voltaire and Belladona. Then have two students volunteer to read the conversation aloud to the class. Did the student authors pick up the special speech patterns of these two characters?

5. This would be an excellent time to have class members prepare a traditional melodrama for the class. *Plays, the Drama Magazine for Young People* would be a good source. Its address is Plays, Inc., 120 Boylston St., Boston, MA 02116. *The Will* by Phyllis J. Perry, April 1993 issue of *Plays*, is one example.

6. This book contains only black-and-white sketches. Have students make a colorful drawing of what happened when the "imaginary forest" appeared on Hurricane Peak. Share these.

📖 *Brother to the Wind*

FICTION

by Mildred Pitts Walter

Illustrated by Diane Dillon and Leo Dillon

New York: Lothrop, Lee & Shepard Books, 1985. 32p.

Primary-grade readers will appreciate this picture book, which is illustrated with muted, full-color drawings.

As the story begins, we meet Emeke, a young African boy who lives in the village of Eronni and herds his family's goats. His grandmother has told him that if he finds Good Snake, the snake can make any wish come true.

Alone in the mountains, Emeke dreams of flying. But when he speaks of it, his friends laugh at him. Emeke wishes for a day off from tending goats so that he can seek Good Snake.

One day, Emeke sees many animals and birds moving toward a nearby tree. Emeke goes to look and sees a huge snake, hanging from the tree. He knows that this is Good Snake.

All the animals except the turtle make a wish. Then it is Emeke's turn. He says he would like to fly. The snake gives him a rock and information about how and when to make and fly a kite.

When Emeke returns to his flock, Hyena offers to herd the goats while Emeke gathers the bamboo and bark he needs for his kite. In the bush, the elephant helps Emeke find the baobab tree. At the watering hole, rhinoceros is waiting for Emeke with three cut kite poles. When the rains come, Emeke stays at home and makes his kite. On the morning of the harvest festival, Emeke takes his kite and goes to the mountain to meet Good Snake. Emeke runs to the edge of the mountain. Like a brother to the wind, he floats down to his people in the village.

Discussion Starters and Multidisciplinary Activities

1. All of the animals that go to see Good Snake make a wish except for turtle. Turtle did not believe in Good Snake and said things without wings do not fly. Ask students why they think turtle was selected to be the doubtful one in this story.

2. Snakes are often regarded as dangerous or evil. Ask students whether or not they were surprised to find that a snake was chosen as the one to grant wishes.

3. Have students comment on whether or not they think that Emeke would have had the courage to talk to Good Snake and make his wish or to jump off the cliff if his grandmother did not believe in Good Snake.

4. The cover of this book shows many things that float or fly—clouds, birds, and butterflies. Have students cut out objects that blow in the wind or fly. Ask them to glue the pictures onto a sheet of construction paper and make a collage.

5. This story is about granting a wish. Ask students to compose their own original short story in which a wish is granted in some unusual way. The story might be fantastic or realistic.

6. People who fly hang gliders leap off cliffs, often near the sea, and soar on the wind. Ask an interested pair of students to research hang gliding. How big are the gliders? Are most purchased or hand-made? What is the longest time that hang gliders have stayed aloft? What is the record for distance? Have these students share pictures and information with the class.

 # *Hurricane*

 FICTION

by David Wiesner

New York: Clarion Books, 1990. 32p. (unnumbered)

Primary-grade readers will enjoy this large-format picture book, which is illustrated with realistic watercolor drawings.

As the story begins, a family has come home from the store just before a storm. While mother puts away groceries, David and George look for their cat, Hannibal. They find the cat and bring him inside. The lights in the house go out, and the family has supper together by the fireplace where everyone feels safe.

When the boys go to bed, the storm has started to ease. They take a hurricane lamp to their room and talk about what it might be like to fly into the eye of a hurricane.

In the morning, the boys find one of their elm trees has blown over into Mr. Wilbur's yard. They start to play among its big limbs and branches. From this point on, illustrations depict the boys' fantasies including a scene in the jungle, a scene set at sea, and a scene in space. Sometimes they simply sit and talk in the tree, which they think of as their private place.

One day men come with chain saws. They cut the fallen tree into small pieces and haul it away. The boys are disappointed. They see that the wind is kicking up and think that maybe there will be another storm. They notice that if the other elm falls, it will land in their yard. On that hopeful note, the story ends.

Discussion Starters and Multidisciplinary Activities

1 Ask students to look for the cat, Hannibal, in each picture. They will find him in all but two of the illustrations.

2 The boys in this story are together a lot, but they never fight and argue. Ask students to explain why these boys get along so well.

3 This story covers three time periods: before the storm, during the storm, and after the storm. Ask students to tell what occurred in each of the three time periods. Then ask which of the time periods they liked best and why.

4 The boys mention that sometimes weather planes fly "into the eye of the hurricane." With the help of your media specialist or adult volunteer, have a few students research this topic. Why would a weather plane want to be in the eye of a hurricane? How do they get there? Have students share what they learn with the class.

5 We do not know whether or not the adults in this story had spoken, but the boys were certainly surprised when Mr. Wilbur arranged to have the tree that fell in his yard cut up and hauled away. Students may raise a question about this. If possible, ask an attorney to visit and explain the rights and responsibilities of people when an object in one yard falls into another. Who is responsible for damages?

6 The cat in this story was called Hannibal. Have a student research Hannibal. Who was he? When did he live and what did he do? Is this a good name for a cat?

 # *Hurricane City*

FICTION

by Sarah Weeks
Illustrated by James Warhola
New York: HarperCollins, 1993. 32p. (unnumbered)

This large-format alphabet book is written in rhymed text with humorous, full-color illustrations. Although alphabet books typically appeal most to kindergarten students, the humor of this book will make it a favorite at other primary-grade levels as well.

The reader is introduced to a family that lives in Hurricane City. At both the beginning and end of the book, the family mentions that, in their city, hurricane season never ends, and that they get every hurricane, large or small.

Hurricane Alvin is the first to sweep through the town. Every other letter of the alphabet, from A to Z, introduces another hurricane such as Hurricane Bertha, Hurricane Chester, and Hurricane Dinah.

With each letter of the alphabet and each new hurricane, there is a special problem for the people in Hurricane City. Hurricane Ethan damages the mailbox, Hurricane Igor causes a flood that fills the swimming pool with mud. Hurricane Laura knocks the steeple off the church. Hurricane Mike comes with hailstones that the local townfolk turn into sno-cones. Hurricane Yvonne knocks over the statue of Abraham Lincoln.

Although the damage from hurricanes shown in the book is real, no one gets hurt, and the damage is always presented in a light and humorous manner.

Discussion Starters and Multidisciplinary Activities

1   Each hurricane shown in the book causes a problem, and each is accompanied by a funny illustration. Ask students which hurricane caused the funniest situation for the people of Hurricane City.

2   The imaginary town in which this story takes place suffers many problems. Go though the pages with students and ask if what is happening in the pictures would happen in real life.

3   One all-American family (two parents, three children, and one dog) are featured throughout the story but are not given names. Have students come up with a funny name related to wind or storms for each character.

4   Real hurricanes are also given names. Have a small number of interested students research hurricanes with the help of an adult volunteer or a media specialist. How many hurricanes hit the United States each year? What were the names of some of these hurricanes? Have students share what they learn with the class.

5   Your class might want to create an alphabet book to present to the kindergarten. Choose a weather-related topic. Have each student pick a letter of the alphabet, write a two-line rhyme, and draw the pictures for that page. The letter *U*, for example, might be for "umbrella." The letter *B* might be for boots to wear in the snow.

6   Have students write an original poem or short story that involves a hurricane. Allow time for students to share their poems and stories with the class.

📖 *Jack and the Whoopee Wind*

FICTION

by Mary Calhoun

Illustrated by Dick Gackenbach

New York: William Morrow, 1987. 32p. (unnumbered)

Primary-grade readers will enjoy this humorous and brightly illustrated picture book.

The main character of the story, Jack, lives in Whoopee, Wyoming, where the wind is so fierce it has blown most of his farm away, and the chickens are bald.

Jack has a dog named Mose, and when the wind seems to torment his dog, Jack gets angry. First, he switches on a big fan and blows at the wind. The wind simply knocks over the fan. Jack gets all the kids in Whoopee to bring their bedsheets. They make a great wind sock to catch the wind, but it keeps blowing.

Jack decides if he could plug up Windy Gap, the wind could not grow so strong. He organizes the cowboys to bring blankets and lariats. They hang a curtain between the hills. The curtain temporarily stops the wind, but then the wind ducks under the curtain.

Jack moves an old outdoor movie screen into the gap to try to stop the wind. The wind blows high over the screen and takes off the top of the town jail. A plan to make a wind tunnel also fails.

Finally, Jack decides the wind needs something to do. He hooks up a lot of windmills to make electricity. The wind keeps so busy with them that not much of it spills over into town. Mose and Jack live happily with the remaining gentle breezes.

Discussion Starters and Multidisciplinary Activities

1. Before the story begins, there is a picture that shows what it is like in Whoopee, Wyoming. What guesses can students make about the story by studying this first picture?

2. Jack gets angry at the wind because of what it does to his dog. Have students discuss how Mose acts after he is blown around by the wind and why he acts this way.

3. Ask students which of Jack's schemes to stop the wind they liked best and why? Did any member of the class have another scheme that might work?

4. When differently shaped things are blown by the wind, they sail differently. Ask students to predict how things will sail when thrown through the air. Record what actually happens. Use a wad of paper, a folded paper airplane, a dollar bill, a feather, a leaf. If dropped, which falls fastest? Why?

5. Wind tunnels are used to test the design of cars and airplanes. Have a pair of students research wind tunnels and the experiments conducted in them. Have students share what they learn with the class.

6. If it is legal in your area, launch helium-filled balloons on a windy day to see just how far and in what direction they travel. Each student should attach a stamped, self-addressed postcard to a short string attached to the balloon. The card asks the finder to fill in the date and the place where the balloon was found and mail it back to the student. On a state map, track where the balloons came down.

Mirandy and Brother Wind

FICTION

by Patricia C. McKissack

Illustrated by Jerry Pinkney

New York: Alfred A. Knopf, 1988. 32p. (unnumbered)

Primary-grade readers will enjoy this large-format picture book, which uses dialect and is illustrated with full-color drawings showing the life of a black farming community.

The story opens in spring. Brother Wind has come swooshing into Ridgetop. Mirandy and Ma Dear are talking about tomorrow night's cakewalk. Mirandy wishes that the wind could be her partner. Ma Dear quotes an old saying that if you can catch the wind, you can make it do your bidding.

The next morning, Mirandy sets out to catch the wind. She asks Grandmama Beasley and the neighbors how to catch the wind. No one can tell her how to do this. Mirandy's friend, a clumsy boy named Ezel, comes to find out why Mirandy is asking about the wind. Clearly he had expected to be her partner at the cakewalk.

Mr. Jessup tells Mirandy to use pepper and a quilt to catch the wind. Mirandy tries this, but it fails. Then Mirandy talks to a conjure woman named Mis Poinsettia. Mis Poinsettia gives directions for catching the wind in a bottle, and she gives her two scarves to wear at the dance. The bottle scheme does not work, but Mirandy catches the wind in the barn.

At the cakewalk, another child makes fun of Ezel's clumsiness. So Mirandy goes back to the wind and whispers what he is to do. Mirandy and Ezel win the junior cakewalk. Everyone watching says they were dancing with the wind.

Discussion Starters and Multidisciplinary Activities

1 Read the author's note describing how the cakewalk was introduced. Ask students to describe any cakewalk that they have participated in or seen.

2 Mirandy tries several ways of catching the wind, but each one fails. Ask students if they thought Mirandy would ever succeed in catching Brother Wind. Why?

3 Ezel was ignored most of the time by Mirandy, but when she heard another girl putting Ezel down, Mirandy quickly came to his defense, saying that she would be his partner. Ask students if this action on Mirandy's part was surprising. Why or why not?

4 If the wind had been Mirandy's partner, the picture of her dancing at the junior cakewalk would have been quite different. Have students make a new drawing in which Mirandy is dancing with Brother Wind.

5 In the poem "Wind Music" by Aileen Fisher, the poet suggests that big winds blow in trees and little winds blow gently on spider webs. Have students write original poems about the wind. They might write about gales and storms or gentle breezes. Share the poems on a bulletin board.

6 A cakewalk is often played in a circle with numbers taped to the floor. Children listen to music and dance around the circle. When the music stops, they stop on a number. Someone pulls a number out of a hat. The child standing on that number wins the cake. The class might enjoy this kind of cakewalk, with cupcakes for prizes, playing it until everyone wins.

📖 *The Turnaround Wind*

FICTION

by Arnold Lobel
New York: Harper & Row, 1988. 32p.

Primary-grade readers will enjoy this large-format picture book with full-color illustrations.

The story begins on a summer afternoon when all the townsfolk are outdoors. Each citizen is paired with another person, object, or animal. There is an organ grinder and his monkey, a man and wife, a nurse and baby, a maiden and soldier, a thief and his bag, a man and his turban, a fisherman and a fish, the mayor and his wife, a farmer with animals, the farmer's wife and a chick, a girl and her dog, a man and his book, a man with a cat, a girl in a hood bringing cookies to her grandmother, a hunter looking for a fox, a lady with a cape and another with an umbrella, a man with his pipe, a lady in a bonnet, an old sailor and his parrot, a girl wearing a bow, an artist with paints, and the King with the Queen.

To everyone's surprise, dark clouds appear, accompanied by a wind that seems to turn the whole world upside down.

Starting on page 10, the student reads the text at the bottom of the page and studies the picture. Then the reader turns the book upside down to read the text at the opposite side of the page and view the picture. For example, the organ grinder on page 10 turns into the sailor's parrot when the book is turned and the picture is viewed upside down.

Finally the wind stops blowing. Everyone goes home to supper except the thief who stays out long after dark.

Discussion Starters and Multidisciplinary Activities

1   Before beginning to read the story, share with the class the title of the book, *The Turnaround Wind*. Ask students to guess what the book might be about.

2   After you have read to the bottom of page 10, ask children to try to recall as many of the characters as they can. List these pairings (king and queen, organ grinder and monkey) on the chalkboard. Then go back and look for any that may have been forgotten.

3   Some of the drawings, viewed right side up and upside down appear to be more successful than others. Have children pick out their favorites and tell why they like these.

4   Trying to draw something that represents a person, animal, or object right side up and upside down is difficult. Give children time to create and share this kind of drawing.

5   The day described in this book might be called a "topsy-turvy" day. The wind turned everything upside down. Ask children to write an original story in which everything is topsy-turvy. Perhaps a toddler has messed up a room or someone has knocked over a jigsaw puzzle. Share the stories.

6   Ask an interested child or group of children to write a few more pages to add to this book. In their addition, have them explain what the thief does and what he finds when he stays out long after dark. Encourage the children to connect their addition with some person, animal, or object that has already appeared in the story.

📖 *Voices on the Wind, Poems for All Seasons*

FICTION

Selected by David Booth
Illustrated by Michele Lemieux
New York: Morrow Junior Books, 1990. 41p.

This book contains a selection of 28 poems by different well-known poets and is illustrated with color drawings. Each of the poems is related to nature and to the seasons of the year. The book, which might enhance study in any section of the present book, is included here because of two poems, "Who Has Seen the Wind?" and "Go Wind."

Christina Rossetti's poem "Who Has Seen the Wind?" is a favorite that some children may recognize. This poem contains two stanzas, eight lines, and uses repetition and end rhyme.

Lilian Moore's poem "Go Wind" is a humorous work. It creates, through its clever use of words, some of the actual sounds of the wind, such as "swoosh" and

"whee." The shape of the poem is also erratic like the wind. Rhyme is most often used at the beginning rather than the end of lines in this poem.

Other poems included in this collection are: "And My Heart Soars," "Who Am I?" "Good Morning," "Down Dip the Branches," "And Suddenly Spring," "Little Seeds," "Bouquet," "Ode to Spring," "Trees," "A Little Song of Life," "That Was Summer," "The Field Mouse," "Browny Bee," "Conversation," "Rain Sizes," "The Lamb," "Autumn Woods," "Fishes Come Bite!" "Autumn Fires," "Taking Off," "Ladybird! Ladybird!" "Under the Ground," "Spiders," "White Fields," "I Am Flying!" and "A Footprint on the Air."

Discussion Starters and Multidisciplinary Activities

1 Read both "Who Has Seen the Wind?" and "Go Wind" with students. Ask which they like best and why.

2 Have students look carefully at the illustration for "Who Has Seen The Wind?" It shows a lighthouse, some islands, and a sailboat. The poem does not mention any of these things. Ask students why they think this illustration was used for this poem.

3 Lilian Moore's poem, "Go Wind" tells the wind not to blow or push the narrator. In Jack Prelutsky's poem, "I Am Flying!" the narrator is actually blowing through the air. Ask students to discuss the humorous elements of Prelutsky's poem.

4 Students could make wind whirlies and hang them on a tree branch. Take plastic lids (margarine tubs, coffee cans, etc.) and punch four equally spaced holes close to outer edge of the lids. With scissors, remove the center. Take four pieces of string one foot in length, Knot each piece to one of the lid holes and then tie the four pieces together in a knot. Tie colored yarn, ribbons, or crepe paper to the plastic circle. When hung, the colored strips will stream out in the wind.

5 Record a group of students trying to create wind sounds (blowing across bottles, etc.). They should share their efforts with the class.

6 Students might want to keep a wind calendar for one month. On each date, they could record the speed and direction of the wind given on the evening news.

The Whirlys and the West Wind

FICTION

by Christine Ross
Boston: Houghton Mifflin, 1993. 28p. (unnumbered)

Primary-grade students will enjoy this easy-to-read picture book with humorous, color illustrations.

The strong west wind carries off Mr. and Mrs. Whirly and the sheet they were holding from the clothesline, leaving behind Flora, Jack, and baby Rose. Because the weather forecast is for continuing gales, it does not seem likely that the two parents will be coming down soon.

The children look at the emergency pages in the phone book but can find no instructions for a west-wind disaster. Within a few days, their house is quite a mess. Toys, clothes, and dishes are left everywhere.

The children decide to take care of themselves by putting a different child in charge each day. On Mondays and Thursdays, Jack is in charge, so all three children go to school. On Tuesdays and Fridays, Flora is in charge, and they play pirates at home all day. On Wednesdays and Sundays, it is baby Rose's turn to be in charge, so they stay home, play, read stories, and go to bed early. On Saturdays they all tidy up.

One day the wind stops, the rain begins to fall, and Mr. and Mrs. Whirly come riding home down the river on a log. The parents are glad to be home and are very impressed with the clean house and the way that the children have taken care of themselves during their absence.

Discussion Starters and Multidisciplinary Activities

1 Before you read the story to the students, show them the first and last pages of the book. On these pages it looks like a story about a very ordinary family. Can students guess from the title of the book what might happen that is not at all ordinary?

2 After hearing the story, ask students to tell what activities they would choose if they were in the Whirly family and were in charge of activities two days each week.

3 Part of this story is real and part is fantasy. Ask students to identify things that occurred in the story that could really happen and some that could not.

4 Children might enjoy a wind chime art project. From a branch or coat hangar they could suspend objects that will make sounds when they move and strike each other. Natural objects like shells and objects from around the house, such keys or short lengths of hollow pipe, could be used.

5 Have a small group of students, working with an adult volunteer or a media specialist, research the Beaufort wind scale and what it measures. Have students share this information with the class.

6 Invite someone to bring an aneroid barometer to class and explain how to read it and what the various readings might mean in terms of weather. If possible, keep the barometer for a few days, take readings, and make a classroom weather prediction. Were you right?

Wind

FICTION

by Monique Felix
Mankato, MN: Creative Editions, 1991. 24p. (unnumbered)

This is a wordless picture book and is suitable for any grade level depending on how it is used. Readers will want to study the pictures carefully to figure out the story. Readers through the elementary grades might be interested in writing a text to accompany the pictures.

As the "story" begins, a mouse enters from the far left side of the page, moves onto the middle of the next page, and begins to look around. On the next several pages, the mouse is busy chewing around the edges of a sheet of paper. The paper seems to have been blocking the full force of the wind.

When the mouse succeeds in chewing all around the paper, the wind begins to blow in full force. With difficulty, the mouse succeeds in folding up the corners of the paper to construct a windmill-type toy. As the mouse chews from the four corners toward the center of the paper, it studies the flight of a bird and the flight of a propeller-driven airplane.

The mouse sticks its tail, like a pin, into a hole in the center of the paper while watching a flock of birds. As he bends the corners of the paper toward the center and over the tip of his pin-like tail, the mouse also sees the blade of a helicopter.

When the paper windmill is complete, the mouse prepares to dive into a picture showing airplanes and parachutes. The mouse leaps, and the paper windmill propels it through the sky.

Discussion Starters and Multidisciplinary Activities

1   After showing the first pages, ask students to guess what the mouse might be looking for. (The mouse shields its eyes with a paw while looking around.)

2   Show the pictures of the mouse gnawing around the sheet of paper. Ask students to guess what the mouse is doing and might want with a sheet of paper. How soon can they tell what the mouse is trying to make?

3   The mouse is using a kind of propeller. What other means of flight are shown in the book?

4   Students might want to make their own windmill toys. The pattern in this book shows them how. Students can work with squares of different colors or add stripes to sheets of white paper. Use a pin to go through the paper windmill and fasten it to a stick. Spin the windmill so that the pinhole is large enough to allow the paper to rotate easily. Outside on a windy day, the windmills should spin quickly.

5   Encourage interested students to write a simple text to go along with the delightful pictures. Students might share these with one another to show the many ways that words can be added and the different interpretations that readers had. The completed stories could be shared with a kindergarten class.

6   Ask a pair of interested students to research house mice and share their findings with the class. How long do they live? What do they eat? How often do they have litters?

◆ *Bridges* ◆

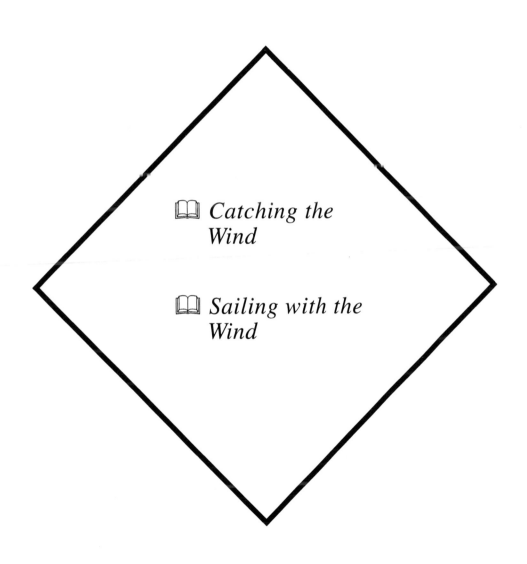

📖 *Catching the Wind*

📖 *Sailing with the Wind*

📖 *Catching the Wind*

BRIDGES

by Joanne Ryder

Illustrated by Michael Rothman

New York: Morrow Junior Books, 1989. 32p. (unnumbered)

Primary-grade students will enjoy this picture book from the Just For a Day Series, in which readers are encouraged to feel that they have been changed into a Canada goose and imagine what it is like to soar over fields and towns. It has realistic, full-color drawings.

This book was selected as a bridge book because it is imaginative, but at the same time contains a lot of factual information about Canada geese.

The story begins in autumn. The wind is calling and changing you. You stretch your wings and fly from your house as a Canada goose. You beat your wings and catch the wind.

You join a dark "V" that is moving under the white clouds. A flock of geese invite you to join them. You fly at the end of the formation over cities and fields until the leader of the flock leads you down from the sky. You land in a small pond and take a long, cool drink. Then you pluck warm, sweet grass to eat. Using your bill, you brush your wind-swept feathers. When you are rested, you all begin to honk and then fly again.

As the geese form a wedge-shaped "V" and chase the warm wind, you turn and begin to head for home, calling good-bye to your new friends. Back home, you glide through the open window right into your bed, where you turn into yourself. On your pillow, you sleep like a bird in its nest.

Possible Topics for Further Student Investigation

1 This story has what is called a circular pattern. The journey begins and ends with a child in her bedroom. This would be a good opportunity to ask interested students to compose a picture book that goes in a circular pattern. Have them plan the book to fit a 24- or 32-page format. Once the text is written, it needs to be divided to fit into the allotted number of pages. Text can go across the top of a page or across the bottom of a page. Illustrations may fit on a single page or may take up a two-page spread. Once the picture books are completed, try to arrange for the students to read them to a kindergarten class.

2 Students who enjoyed this story might also like to read *Close Your Eyes* by Jean Marzollo, with pictures by Susan Jeffers. A father tries to put a child to sleep and encourages the child to rest by explaining that if you have your eyes closed, you can imagine, and through imagination, you can visit with anyone, anywhere. Ask a pair of students to read *Close Your Eyes* and make a book report to share with the class.

3 Canada geese have striking markings, and the markings are surprisingly uniform from one bird to the next. Encourage students to study the pictures in this book and then to make their own drawing that might illustrate a section of the text. Students should use any medium that they prefer, and may choose any section of the book to illustrate, but be sure to have them include at least one Canada goose. When the pictures are finished, you might want to display them on a bulletin board for others to enjoy.

Sailing with the Wind

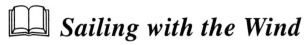

BRIDGES

by Thomas Locker

New York: Dial Books, 1986. 32p. (unnumbered)

In this picture book, a young girl joins her uncle on a sailing trip and learns about the beauty of the ocean. Told in the first person, it is illustrated with magnificent oil paintings. The simple text will appeal to primary-grade children. Older students might also enjoy studying the illustrations.

This is a bridge book, or companion piece to *Catching the Wind* in which the reader experiences the wind by imagining flying. In this book, the wind is experienced by imagining sailing on the water.

Uncle Jack, who works on a big ship and sails all over the world, is coming to visit. Uncle Jack has promised Elizabeth that one day they will sail down the river to the ocean. After he arrives, it is decided that the next day Elizabeth will go sailing with Uncle Jack.

They wake up early, get into the boat, and are carried by the river's current. The sails fill with wind and they pick up speed. They stop for a picnic on a little island before sailing into the bay and out on the ocean. Uncle Jack thinks a storm is brewing, so they head back. The rain comes pouring down on them and Elizabeth bails rainwater out of the boat. The rain stops just before they reach the cove and home.

Uncle Jack stays for one week but becomes restless. He promises to return in a couple of years and take Elizabeth on another adventure.

Possible Topics for Further Student Investigation

1 Find and read some "ocean poems" to the students. You might have your own favorites, but you could also seek: "Out of the Sea Early" or "Beginning to Squall" by May Swanson; "With Kit, Age 7, At the Beach" by William Stafford; and "Sand Dunes" by Robert Frost. After you read a poem, ask students to discuss it. What pictures do they form in their minds? Do they see the ocean in many different moods through these poems? Then ask students to write original ocean poems. These may be rhymed or unrhymed. Students might wish to illustrate their poems. Include these poems and pictures on a bulletin board.

2 There are many different kinds of sailboats. Your media specialist would be helpful in securing and sharing with a small group of interested students some magazines and books that have pictures and information about boats. Once students become familiar with different boats, have them share their information with class members in an oral report.

3 There are several famous races that are held each year for different kinds of boats. A media specialist will be helpful to a small group of students who wish to research this topic. For the races that they choose, have the students find out when and where each race is held, the distance covered, some of the winning times, and information about the crews, including which country they represented. Ask the students to prepare a chart in which they include the names of some boat races and some specific information about each one to share with the class.

Windy Days

Nonfiction Connections

- 📖 *The Air I Breathe*
- 📖 *Catch the Wind! All About Kites*
- 📖 *Changes in the Wind: Earth's Shifting Climate*
- 📖 *Facts on Water, Wind and Solar Power*
- 📖 *Flight*
- 📖 *Hot-Air Ballooning*
- 📖 *Projects with Flight*
- 📖 *Weather*
- 📖 *The Weather Sky*
- 📖 *Wind*
- 📖 *Wind & Water Power*
- 📖 *Wind Power*

 # *The Air I Breathe*

NONFICTION CONNECTIONS

by Bobbie Kalman and Janine Schaub
New York: Crabtree, 1993. 32p.

This large-format book will be enjoyed by students in grades two through four. It is part of The Primary Ecology Series and is illustrated with color charts and photographs.

This book begins with a discussion of air as the breath of life. The text explains that air is essential to life and that it carries smells, tiny particles, and even large objects. We use air in many ways. It heats and cools us, dries our clothes, and lets us sail boats. Blown through an instrument, it makes beautiful sounds. It carries the seeds of plants and turns windmills to generate power.

After this introduction, there is a section on the body's needs, how we breathe, how air travels through the windpipe, and how it is carried by blood throughout the body. A large chart shows the windpipe, lung, bronchioles, and diaphragm. Pictures and text show how to do power breathing.

The next section uses diagrams to explain and show how air lets you hear and how you can smell air.

The text emphasizes that although air travels all over the planet, it never leaves the atmosphere. Wind is caused when cool and warm air change places. Included is a discussion of windchill factor, hurricanes, funnels, and the Beaufort scale, as well as allergies, asthma, lung diseases, air pollution, and ozone.

Possible Topics for Further Student Investigation

1 This might be a good time to invite your physical education teacher or school nurse to visit the classroom and discuss breathing and healthy lungs. Correct posture and deep breathing could be demonstrated. This might also be an appropriate time to discuss what smoking cigarettes or inhaling second-hand smoke can do to injure lungs.

2 The word "air" is used to suggest a variety of meanings. Ask each student to write a page of conversation between two characters. In the conversation, each character should use the word "air" at least twice and in different ways. For example, one character might accuse the other of "putting on airs" by walking past and ignoring her. The other character might maintain she did not see her friend because she was "walking on air" after learning she had aced a math test. Take time to share the dialogue.

3 This book explains that plants in the classroom or at home are not only attractive but also help keep the air fresh. Have an interested student carry out the following activity to show that a plant will give off oxygen when it makes food from sunlight. Cut a shoot of Canadian pondweed and put it in a clean mayonnaise jar that is filled with water. Place the jar with the pondweed in a sunny window in the classroom. Students will be able to observe bubbles of oxygen rising in the water. Then, if you move the jar of pondweed out of the sunlight, the bubbles will cease.

📖 *Catch the Wind! All About Kites*

NONFICTION CONNECTIONS

by Gail Gibbons

Boston: Little, Brown, 1989. 32p. (unnumbered)

This book uses the framework of two children visiting a kite shop to provide factual information. There are simple, full-color illustrations. The book will be enjoyed by primary-grade students.

As the story begins, Ike, the owner of the kite shop, shares information with the children. He explains that historians believe that the Chinese flew the very first kites more than 3,000 years ago. He adds that kites have been used not only for fun, but also for religious festivals, for science experiments, for carrying weather-measuring devices, and for military signaling.

The author provides other informa tion about Benjamin Franklin's kite experiments in 1752, the invention of the box kite by Lawrence Hargrave in 1893, and the early kite experiments of Wilbur and Orville Wright prior to building and flying their first airplane at Kitty Hawk in 1903.

There are detailed descriptions of several kinds of kites: flat, bowed, boxed, compound, triangular, delta, sled, parachute, wind sock, and parafoils.

After Katie and Sam buy kites, Ike invites them to attend a kite festival. The two children attend and see all kinds of kites flying above the meadow. They launch their kites.

The final three pages of the book are devoted to descriptions of how to make your own flat kite, launch it, and bring down the kite. Safety tips are also provided.

Possible Topics for Further Student Investigation

1   Students who read this book will probably be interested in building a kite. It could be a class project, with each student building a kite. Set aside time on a clear day when the wind is blowing from 8 to 20 miles per hour. Students could follow the book's directions for kite building, consult another book, or visit a hobby or kite shop for plans and materials. This project requires a large, open, safe place outdoors for the kite festival. The area needs to be free of power lines and other obstacles.

2   Students interested in flight will want to learn more about Orville and Wilbur Wright. Encourage a pair of interested students to do research on these two men. When and where did they live? When did they fly the first airplane? What did it look like? What improvements did they make to their first design? Ask these students to share their information with the class.

3   The principle of "lift" discussed in this book pertains both to kites and to airplanes. There are a number of good books on designing paper airplanes. Bring some of these books to class for an interest center. Encourage interested students to design different paper airplanes and test these designs. Which planes travel the greatest distance and remain airborne the longest? These students might go outside with classmates and demonstrate some of their paper airplane designs.

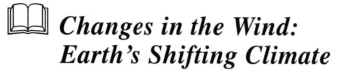

Changes in the Wind: Earth's Shifting Climate

by Margery Facklam and Howard Facklam
San Diego, CA: Harcourt Brace Jovanovich, 1986. 128p.

NONFICTION CONNECTIONS

This book is mostly text, illustrated with diagrams and black-and-white photographs. It is appropriate for fourth- and fifth-grade readers.

The authors explain the complex interaction between climate and natural forces such as the Sun, ocean, volcanoes, forests, and ice caps. The text also tells how people affect climate.

The world's weather is like a giant web. If the monsoons are late in the Far East, there may be a cold snap in Ohio. If a volcano erupts in Mexico, the wheat crop may fail in Europe.

Like a tunnel of wind, the jet stream flows in a series of loops. Wherever there are extreme temperature differences, the jet stream is fastest. These high air currents are important in plotting air traffic and in predicting weather.

The text explains that winds are the atmosphere in motion. Warm air expands and rises while cool air sinks. Since our earth spins toward the east, air and water in the Northern Hemisphere veer to the right and, below the equator, veer to the left. Because the earth is not smooth, mountains and valleys change the direction of winds.

Additional chapters focus on the greenhouse effect and ice age predictions; volcano, forest, solar, and food connections; and the possibility of man-made winter on our planet.

Possible Topics for Further Student Investigation

1 Ask an interested student to read chapter 4, which deals with the greenhouse effect prediction and do additional research. This student should write a paper and include the titles and dates of books and magazines that were consulted. The paper should explain clearly what the "greenhouse effect" is. What makes it difficult to make accurate predictions about it? How are computer models being used by climatologists to indicate changes in the weather?

2 Ask a small group of students to study the food connection in chapter 10 of this book. Have them practice sharing information in a round-table discussion like a television talk show. Each student will be responsible for a certain point of view and for sharing information about changes in weather, climate, droughts, famines, and so on. When they are ready, have this group share what they have learned in a talk show format with the rest of the class.

3 Scientists have shown that forests play a vital role in the world's weather. Acid rain and the deforestation of tropical rain forests pose huge problems for people. If you have access to someone from a college, a university, or governmental agency that deals in such matters, arrange for a guest speaker to visit the class and share information. If pictures or slides will be available, be sure to make arrangements ahead of time so that slide projectors, video equipment, and so on is available. The class might prepare and submit specific questions ahead of time.

 *Facts on Water, Wind and Solar Power*

by Guy Arnold

New York: Franklin Watts, 1990. 32p.

This is a large-format book, illustrated with drawings and color photographs, appropriate for students in grades two through four. It contains sections on "Renewable Energy," "Wind Power," "Wind on Water," "Water Power," "Tidal Power," "Solar Power," and "World Climates." It includes a glossary.

The most interesting sections on "Windy Days" deal with wind power and wind on water. In the introduction to the book, the author explains that, at present, most of the world's energy comes from fossil fuels or nuclear reactors. As fossil fuels are depleted, it is increasingly important to harness renewable solar, wind, and water power sources.

In the section on wind power, readers learn that, since ancient times, wind has been used to drive windmills on land and sailing vessels at sea. Although wind power is not currently highly developed, the potential amount of energy available from this source is enormous.

Large-scale attempts to use windmills to generate electricity have not been successful. It requires a generator to be connected directly to the shaft of the windmill blades to be efficient. The electricity then passes to a control house. Such machinery can be noisy. The number of windmills required to provide power for a town or small city can spoil the landscape.

Possible Topics for Further Student Investigation

1 Windmills have been used successfully on Britain's western coasts to produce one-third of the needed energy. Ask a small group of interested students to research the current use of windmills to produce energy. Are there windmill farms anywhere in the United States? Where are they located? How much energy do they produce? What are the major problems associated with windmill farms throughout the world? Where are they used most successfully? Have students share their information in a report to the class.

2 Wind power is also used to move ships at sea. There is a picture and discussion on pages 12 and 13 telling how a Japanese tanker has computer-operated aluminum sails which save ten percent of its engine's fuel consumption. Have a small group of interested students do further research on this. How practical and widespread is the use of these aluminum sails? Are there disadvantages as well as advantages to using them? Have students share what they learn with the class.

3 One of the problems associated with the world's reliance on fossil fuels is that a number of oil spills have occurred, causing widespread damage to beaches, fish, and birds. Some of these oil spills received a lot of publicity. Have a small group of interested students research oil spills. Where and when did the most costly occur? How do people deal with an oil spill? Students should share what they learn with the class.

 ## *Flight*

by Malcolm Dixon
Illustrated by Stephen Wheele
New York: Bookwright Press, 1991. 48p.

Third- through fifth-grade readers will enjoy this book from the series called T.E.C.H.N.O.L.O.G.Y. P.R.O.J.E.C.T.S. The activity-based series encourages readers to explore basic design and technology concepts. The book is illustrated with color drawings and photographs.

Sections are devoted to: air and lift, making an airfoil, watching birds fly, making a model insect, making a parachute, making paper spinners, making a hot-air balloon, making and flying a kite, building a glider, making a hang glider, rubber-band power, making a powered aircraft, making a model helicopter and a jet-propelled cable car, making a delta-wing glider, and making a water rocket.

The author explains how flight has developed from simple kites and hot-air balloons to modern jets. The experiments in the book are designed to give readers an understanding of the basic principles of flight.

Some of the experiments, such as the demonstration of moving air and lift, are very simple and require minimal supplies. Others, such as making a powered aircraft, require supplies such as a plastic airplane propeller, balsa wood, plastic pipe, rubber bands, and balsa cement.

Each experiment or project is accompanied by related text and either drawings or photographs.

Possible Topics for Further Student Investigation

1   One of the projects in this book which requires adult supervision and observance of all safety precautions is the construction of a water rocket. The teacher or an adult volunteer might want to demonstrate this project to the class. Required materials are two empty, clean, plastic drink bottles, rubber cork, two rubber bands, a football inflator valve, and several bicycle pump connectors. Complete directions are given on page 41 of the book.

2   If there is a local airport, this might be a good time to arrange a visit. Ask if the airport provides tours for school groups. If such a trip is possible, have students discuss what they want to see and discover during their visit. A student should be responsible for recording this information and should send it in advance to the person who will conduct the tour. Students should also be responsible for a follow-up thank you letter.

3   Many plants have seeds that fly in the wind. Among these are the winged fruits of the sycamore and the parachute-like seeds of the dandelion. Ask a small group of interested students to research seeds and the ways that they travel. Have students collect as many kinds of seeds as possible. They should attach each seed to an index card indicating the plant it came from and how it moves from place to place. When they have enough information, students could make a display in the classroom and share their information.

Hot-Air Ballooning

by Charles Coombs
New York: William Morrow, 1981. 128p.

NONFICTION
CONNECTIONS

This book is mostly text and is illustrated with black-and-white photographs. It contains a useful glossary. It is appropriate for students in grades three through five.

Depending upon where you live, students may or may not be familiar with seeing hot-air balloons. Even those who have not been close to hot-air balloons have probably seen some enormous balloons inflated for displays at malls or as part of a huge parade.

This book discusses the first hot-air balloon flights by early aeronauts in France and the changes and dangers associated with the development of hydrogen-filled balloons. The experimentation with light-weight, gasoline-fueled internal-combustion engines at the end of the nineteenth century is discussed in some detail. Included is the work of Count von Zeppelin and the rigid aluminum structure that housed hydrogen-filled bags as well as the experiments of the Wright brothers to fly a heavier-than-air machine at Kitty Hawk.

Readers will learn about the manufacture and construction of hot-air balloons, their baskets, equipment, training, and safety. There is information on pilot's licenses, pre-flight planning and procedures, flying in a hot-air balloon, and landing. The text also discusses the Balloon Federation of America, the National Aeronautic Association, and the worldwide Federation Aeronautique Internationale.

Possible Topics for Further Student Investigation

1 Because of the many significant names associated with early flight, this might make a good opportunity to introduce students to biographies and historical research. Among those that may be available are books or articles dealing with the Wright Brothers, Henry Cavendish, Jacques Charles, Francois Pilatre de Rozier, Madame Thible, and Count von Zeppelin. Have a group of students work with a media specialist to study someone in the general area of flight and share what they learn with the class.

2 A pair of students might be interested in researching and constructing a time line for the classroom which will include the dates of significant events that occurred in the history of humans' attempts to fly. Some illustrations might be added to the time line to make it more attractive and interesting. The completed time line could be mounted in the classroom.

3 On May 6, 1937 at Lakehurst, New Jersey, the Hindenburg, a magnificent dirigible that was almost three times the length of a standard football field, burst into flames and crashed. Crew and passengers jumped and tried to save their lives, but 33 people died in the crash. Much has been written about this tragedy. Have an interested student research this topic and gather background information. Have that student share the information with the class in the form of an in-depth evening-news television report.

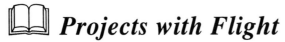 *Projects with Flight*

**NONFICTION
CONNECTIONS**

by John Williams

Illustrated by Malcolm S. Walker

Milwaukee: Gareth Stevens Children's Books, 1992. 32p.

This book is part of the Simple Science Projects series and is approximately half text and half color drawings and photographs. It will be of interest to students in grades two through four.

The book centers on aspects of flight including: flying machines, paper airplanes, gliders, going gliding, helicopters, nature's spinners, minigliders, catapults, birds, kites, and kite flying. It also contains information about supplies needed to complete the projects outlined, a bibliography for more information, and places to write for science supply catalogs.

Each book project is tied to related text. For example, the fact that Leonardo da Vinci used nature as his guide and designed his model gliders from what he learned about birds, is the introduction to making a da Vinci–style miniglider. The glider is made from plastic straws and poster board using scissors, tape, and modeling clay.

A section introduces helicopters and their rotor blades that spin and lift the helicopter off the ground. The accompanying project details a simple paper helicopter constructed from cardboard cut and bent to create rotor blades.

Directions for projects are clear, and safety is stressed.

Possible Topics for Further Student Investigation

1 Many students enjoy designing and flying paper airplanes. Few have ever shot their paper airplanes into the air with a catapult. A pair of students, under the guidance of an adult supervisor could make two catapults following the directions on page 21 of *Projects with Flight*. These catapults could then be used to launch paper airplanes. The class might divide into two groups and take turns shooting their planes from the catapults and observing flight distance.

2 If the paper airplanes are a success, students might like to experiment with making gliders from balsa wood and foam tubings. The directions are given on page 9 of *Projects with Flight*. (Depending on students' age and skill, pieces of balsa and tubing could be precut by an adult, or supervised students could do their own cutting.) The information on page 10 about properly balancing the glider is crucial to success in flight. Students could put their names on the wings and decorate them before taking the gliders out for test flights.

3 A group of students might want to research the requirements for earning a glider pilot license. Have these students seek out information such as license requirements, the closest school where they could take lessons, tow fees, and other information. Have them share this information with the class. If possible, invite a licensed glider pilot to visit the class and share information about soaring.

Weather

by Michael Cooper
Illustrated by Mike Atkinson
Vero Beach, FL: Rourke, 1984. 64p.

This small book is part of a scientific and technical series of books, "The Rourke Guides." All measurements are shown in the metric system with U.S. equivalents. It is illustrated with color charts and drawings. This book is suitable for use by students in grades three through five.

This book contains six chapters: "What Is Weather?" "Elements of Weather"; "Weather Patterns"; "Weather Disasters"; "Weather Forecasts"; and "Controlling the Weather." Of particular interest to students is the information about air circulation, air streams, Beaufort scale, cyclones, doldrums, Dust Bowl, Foehn winds, hurricanes, jet streams, planetary winds, pressure, prevailing winds, sea breezes, tornadoes, trade winds, typhoons, twisters, and wind belts.

The section on pressure and wind explains that wind is simply air blowing from one of high pressure to an area of low pressure. Sea breezes are the result of land heating and cooling more rapidly than the sea, so that during the day, the rapidly heated air above the land rises, creating an area of low pressure. A current of cooler air moves in from the sea to replace the rising air, and this is called a sea breeze.

There is a section on hurricanes, tornadoes, and also information about instruments to measure wind velocity.

Possible Topics for Further Student Investigation

1   The section on controlling the weather gives interesting information about preventing hailstorm damage to crops in Russia and China by shooting anti-hail shells filled with chemicals into hail clouds. In other places, cloud seeding is used to try to initiate rain. Ask a pair of interested students to do more research with the help of an adult media specialist. They should share with the class what they learn and include a list of books, magazines, or pamphlets that they consulted.

2   There is a brief section on synoptic charts. Weather information is collected from observers around the world and at fixed times, sent to regional stations and then to major centers, and used in the preparation of a 24-hour weather forecast. With the help of a media specialist, ask a pair of students to research this topic. Where is the closest regional weather station? Would it be possible to get a piece of a synoptic chart? How are these mathematical charts turned into simplified maps for the public? Students should share what they learn with the class.

3   Three points on a Beaufort wind scale are shown on page 15 of *Weather*. Have an interested pair of students research and then make a large chart that represents the 12 points on the Beaufort scale and hang this on a bulletin board. Have students explain their chart to the class.

The Weather Sky

by Bruce McMillan
New York: Farrar, Straus & Giroux, 1991. 40p.

NONFICTION
CONNECTIONS

Students in grades three through five will enjoy this large-format book illustrated with charts and photographs.

The book begins with a weather map and information about air masses. The text explains that the "weather zone" is the lowest layer of the earth's atmosphere. It is made up of air masses that extend from the ground to about 10 miles high. Cold, warm, and stationary fronts are discussed.

Most of the book deals with clouds. With exceptions, they are classified from lowest to highest and are: stratus, cumulus, cumulus congestus, stratocumulus, nimbostratus altocumulus, towering cumulus, altostratus, cumulonimbus, cirrostratus, cirrus, and cumulonimbus capillatus.

The author briefly explains the Latin-based names of the clouds.

Clouds are useful in weather forecasting because the clouds associated with fronts usually occur in a predictable sequence. Photographs are used to show scenes such as a typical summer day, the approach of a warm front, and an autumn sky with cool, most air.

In addition to text and photographs, two charts appear on most pages. One places the clouds by height, from ground level to 40,000 feet up. Another shows the viewing spot and a portion of the local weather map. Included is a helpful glossary.

Possible Topics for Further Student Investigation

1. Have a student collect the weather maps from a home-town or a nearby city's newspaper for a two-week period. Have the student post these maps on a bulletin board. Beneath each of these posted weather maps, have the student record actual weather data such as high and low temperatures, barometric reading, and whether it was a sunny, rainy, windy, or cloudy day. From the posted information, could students see that the weather maps were useful in predicting weather?

2. If a student is interested in photography, have that student make a series of cloud photographs to place on a bulletin board and to share with the class. If possible, the photos should be taken from the same location(s) and the photographer should include time and date and indicate North in each photo. Using information in this and other books, can the student photographer, with help from other class members, name the pictured clouds?

3. Using a large sheet of blue construction paper and some white cotton balls, ask a pair of students to make a chart to mount in the classroom during your weather unit. The chart should show the kinds of clouds, their names, and a brief explanation. A stratus cloud, for example, will be shown as a flat, layered cloud with its Latin name meaning "spread out," while cumulus clouds will be shown as a bunch of puffy-shaped clouds with its Latin name meaning "heap."

 ## *Wind*

by Joy Palmer
Austin, TX: Raintree Steck-Vaughn, 1993. 32p.

This is part of a series of books called First Starts, a general science series for children that explores topics such as deserts, oceans, volcanoes, and rain forests. There is a simple text, appropriate for second- and third-graders, and the book is illustrated with color drawings and photographs.

The book begins with a discussion of wind and how is it measured. The text explains that wind occurs when air flows from an area of high pressure to one of low pressure. The Beaufort scale is used to estimate wind speed. This scale goes from 0, which means that there is no wind, to 12, which means that there is a hurricane. A force of 6 means that there is a strong breeze that could blow an umbrella inside out.

Hurricanes, tornadoes, winds at sea, dust, and sandstorms are discussed next. Photographs show some of the destruction and devastation such winds can cause.

The next section tells how plants survive wind and how wind carries pollen. Birds and animals also use the wind and have some special adaptations to protect themselves against wind (camels have two sets of eyelashes).

The final section describes how people design buildings and bridges to withstand wind, how they use wind energy, and how they enjoy the wind by sailing and flying kites. There is a short section for things to do, and the book concludes with a glossary.

Possible Topics for Further Student Investigation

1   This book suggests making a simple weather vane. This might make an interesting classroom project if it can be placed so that students can check it and use the data in a classroom weather station. A compass needs to be used to determine the wind direction. Compass points need to be marked for the spot or spots where weather vanes are used. One way of making the weather vane is to fill a bottle with sand, cork it, push a knitting needle into the cork, and place a long, loose pen top over the top of the needle. Then securely tape a paper arrow to the pen top which will spin in the wind.

2   In some parts of the country, there are parks and monuments famous for the fantastic rock formations formed by blowing wind. Ask a pair of students who are interested in this topic to gather information about one of these areas and share an illustrated travelogue describing what a visitor might expect to see.

3   Tornadoes are violent winds that touch the earth and cause damage while whirling at great speed. Ask an interested student to read detailed reports of a tornado that occurred somewhere in the United States. Have that student write up the information in an exciting way and deliver it to that class in the form of an evening-news bulletin. Who, what, why, when and where, as well as exciting details should be included in the student "broadcast."

📖 *Wind & Water Power*

by Clint Twist
New York: Gloucester Press, 1992. 32p.

This book is part of the World About Us series, which introduces young readers to environmental problems. The book is approximately half text and half colored illustrations. It will appeal to second-through fourth-grade readers.

This book focuses on alternative energy sources and emphasizes that the world uses more energy each year, especially in the form of electricity. Fuels used for generating electricity often produce pollution. Wind and water power, by contrast, are cleaner and renewable energy sources.

Wind has been used for thousands of years to enable ships to sail and to turn windmills that perform tasks such as grinding corn. There is a detailed diagram of a modern windmill—a wind turbine—which is used today to produce electricity.

Wind "farms" have large numbers of wind turbines (used in some places such as California), but there are problems associated with them. They take up a large area of land, look ugly, create noise, and can cause television interference.

Water is easier to harness. Waterwheels can be built wherever there is a suitable stream; dams can be built to stop the flow of water and generate electricity. In the future, people will use more alternative energy sources including wind turbines, hydroelectric power plants, solar power, and even converting the movement of waves into electricity.

Possible Topics for Further Student Investigation

1 This book points out that as fossil-fuel resources are exhausted, humans will need alternative energy sources. Have a small group of students do research on nonrenewable energy sources: coal, oil, and gas. From the data they find, have these students prepare charts and graphs explaining the current state of these natural resources, expected rates of depletion, and dates when we are predicted to run out of these fuels. Students should also use a world map to show the location of existing large deposits of coal, oil, and gas.

2 Another energy source is nuclear power. One of the problems with nuclear power is that waste products remain dangerous for many thousand of years. In recent years, certain areas have become receiving sites for waste nuclear fuel. Some people protest having these wastes buried in their states. Others are concerned about the dangers of transporting such hazardous waste. Ask a pair of interested students to research nuclear waste disposal and transportation and share what they learn with the class.

3 Sails on sailing ships are complex and interesting. Invite a sailor to visit the class and discuss various kinds of sailing vessels. How are the sails adjusted to take advantage of wind power? If possible, have the guest speaker use models, charts, films, or videos to illustrate the discussion.

 *Wind Power*

by Mike Cross

Illustrated by Ron Hayward Associates

New York: Gloucester Press, 1985. 32p.

This book is part of a series called Energy Today. This series covers today's major energy resources. It is approximately half text and is illustrated with color drawings and photographs. It will appeal to students in grades two through four.

The introduction explains that we need energy for all sorts of things and that if we can successfully harness the wind, we will have a renewable energy source. Individual sections include information about: energy from the wind, catching the wind, Savonius rotor, wind pumps, wind turbines, Darrieus, wind farms, Sea Clams, wave rafts, and sail power. The book also includes fact files and a glossary.

Old-fashioned windmills have provided power to pump water and grind corn, but they are too small to make large amounts of electricity. Engineers are currently designing and testing wind turbines in the hope that they will provide a major source of electricity. Both traditional windmills and modern turbines work in similar ways. They must be able to adjust to wind speed or strong gusts may damage them.

Other power sources are discussed. The Savonius rotor is used in developing countries. Darrieus wind turbines reflect a new design. Long barriers called Sea Clams and wave rafts rely on the power of waves along the shores of oceans and lakes.

Possible Topics for Further Student Investigation

1 A student who is interested in the Savonius rotor could make a small model by studying the diagram on page 10 of *Wind Power*. Rather than use a tin can with its sharp metal edges, the student could use a plastic soda pop bottle for the "oil drum." A dowel could be used for the spindle and a tongue depressor for the tie bar. By blowing into the device, the student could demonstrate for the class how this type of rotor works.

2 Wind currents are caused by differences between warm and cool air. A simple science experiment in the classroom can help illustrate this. Take an empty soda bottle and pass it around so that students can feel its temperature. Then place the soda bottle into a bucket of ice water and leave it there for a few minutes. Fasten a balloon onto the empty bottle. Pass the bottle around again. At first it will feel cool. Gradually it will be warmed by students' hands. As it is warmed, the balloon may begin to inflate. Place the bottle into a bucket of hot water. The balloon inflates. If the bottle is placed back into cold water, the balloon deflates. Explain that a sort of wind current has been created in the bottle.

3 Read the fanciful poem "The Moon's the North Wind's Cooky" by Vachel Lindsay. Ask students to write some original poems in which the wind is associated with some other object such as waves, windmills, treetops, laundry on a clothesline, and so on. Have students illustrate their poems and display them on a bulletin board.

Part III

Snowy Days

Snowy Days

● FICTION ●

- 📖 *Birthday Blizzard*
- 📖 *The Black Snowman*
- 📖 *Brrr!*
- 📖 *Dogteam*
- 📖 *First Snow*
- 📖 *Geraldine's Big Snow*
- 📖 *The Key into Winter*

- 📖 *Look! Snow!*
- 📖 *Out on the Ice in the Middle of the Bay*
- 📖 *Snow Company*
- 📖 *Snow Toward Evening: A Year in a River Valley: Nature Poems*
- 📖 *When the Mountain Sings*

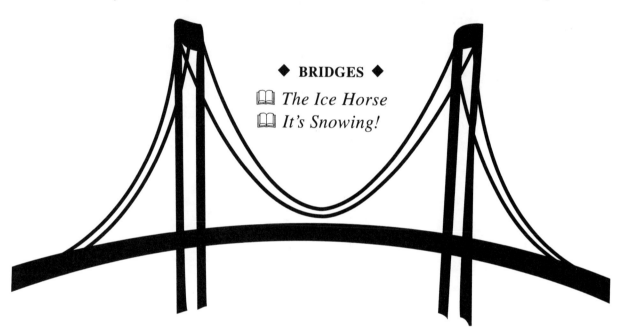

◆ BRIDGES ◆

- 📖 *The Ice Horse*
- 📖 *It's Snowing!*

■ NONFICTION CONNECTIONS ■

- 📖 *Glaciers*
- 📖 *High in the Wind: The Snow Geese*
- 📖 *The Ice Ages*
- 📖 *Ice Skating Is for Me*
- 📖 *Icebergs, Titans of the Oceans*

- 📖 *Icebergs and Glaciers*
- 📖 *Snow*
- 📖 *Snow and Ice*
- 📖 *Snow Is Falling*
- 📖 *Snow Sports*
- 📖 *Weather & Climate*
- 📖 *Winter Weather*

—OTHER TOPICS TO EXPLORE—

—Antarctic	—Arctic	—Avalanche	—Ice
—Ice skating	—Skiing	—Sledding	—Sled dogs
—Snow boarding	—Snowflakes	—Snow removal	—Winter Olympics

Snowy Days

● *Fiction* ●

- 📖 *Birthday Blizzard*
- 📖 *The Black Snowman*
- 📖 *Brrr!*
- 📖 *Dogteam*
- 📖 *First Snow*
- 📖 *Geraldine's Big Snow*
- 📖 *The Key into Winter*
- 📖 *Look! Snow!*
- 📖 *Out on the Ice in the Middle of the Bay*
- 📖 *Snow Company*
- 📖 *Snow Toward Evening: A Year in a River Valley: Nature Poems*
- 📖 *When the Mountain Sings*

 # Birthday Blizzard

FICTION

by Bonnie Pryor
Illustrated by Molly Delaney
New York: Morrow Junior Books, 1993. 32p. (unnumbered)

This picture book, with its full-color, playful illustrations, will appeal to primary-grade readers.

The night before Jamie's birthday, a blizzard roars through town. It is still snowing the next morning. Electricity and phones are out. Daddy puts wood in the fireplace and finds the camp stove. Jamie is grumbly. No one will come to her party.

Jamie and her father go next door to check on Mr. and Mrs. Piper and their two sturdy work horses. They give the horses food and water and notice some small tracks, like a dog's, in the snow. The Piper's do not have a fireplace to keep them warm, so they come home with Jamie and her father.

The Piper's say that someone dumped a puppy in their pasture, but they could not catch him. Later, a young couple and their baby, whose car is stuck in a snow drift, join them. Then Mr. and Mrs. Mac-Donald, with Laura and Tim, drop in. They got caught in the storm on their way home from a visit to Grandma's for Christmas. Even the snowplow driver gets stuck and comes inside. Mother brings out the birthday cake, and they play games. The guests find little things to give Jamie. Then the puppy scratches at the door. Jamie names the puppy Blizzard. The storm stops. Power is restored, and the new friends leave. It was a great birthday after all!

Discussion Starters and Multidisciplinary Activities

1 Jamie wishes that her birthday were in the summer. But sometimes people with summer birthdays complain that all their school friends are away on vacation. Ask students to pick the date of their birthday. When would it be, and why?

2 When power fails in winter, it is dark, cold and inconvenient. Ask students to share adventures that they may have had during a power outage.

3 Jamie had a fine birthday after all and even got a new puppy. Ask students if they think Jamie would have traded her Blizzard Birthday for an ordinary birthday party. Why or why not?

4 In this story, a new pet is introduced to the family, a dog that appeared to have been dumped in a farmer's pasture because its owners did not want it or could not care for it. There are many homeless pets. Invite someone from your local Humane Society or Animal Shelter to come to class and talk about the care of pets and the kind of work that is done at the Humane Society.

5 Pets sometimes get their names because of some special event. In this story, the puppy was called "Blizzard" because of the snowstorm that was raging when this family found him. Ask students to write an original short story. In the story, have a new pet join a family. Give the pet an unusual name, a name connected in some way with the events in the story.

6 Let students add a picture to this book—the scene in Jamie's kitchen the morning after her birthday party.

📖 *The Black Snowman*

FICTION

by Phil Mendez
Illustrated by Carole Byard
New York: Scholastic, 1989. 48p. (unnumbered)

This is a long picture book with full-color illustrations. It will be enjoyed by primary-grade students.

The story begins long ago with a legend about a village in western Africa. There, an old storyteller puts on a magic kente, or brightly colored cloth, which restores his memory. The villagers are sold into slavery and go to America. The kente cloth is sold, frayed, and discarded, but it still possesses some magic.

When the main story begins, Jacob makes a scene with his mother at breakfast in front of his brother Peewee. Jacob says they will not go Christmas shopping and will get old clothes from the Salvation Army. He says he hates being black.

The boys go outside and make a black snowman out of dirty snow. Peewee gives the snowman an old hat and buttons for eyes. He drapes the old kente cloth around the snowman's shoulders. The magic of the kente brings the snowman alive.

That night, Peewee tells his plan to collect empty bottles to get enough money to buy Mama a Christmas present. Later, Jacob sneaks outside, and the black snowman tells him about the brave Africans from whom he has descended.

The next day, Jacob and the snowman with the kente cloth rescue Peewee from a burning building. Later, a fireman picks up the piece of cloth and takes it home to his daughter.

Discussion Starters and Multidisciplinary Activities

1 Among other things, Jacob hates hand-me-downs and chipped, worn-out things like his lamp. But some people love old things that have been handed down in the family. Ask students if they have some old object with an interesting history that they would like to tell about.

2 Mama says that Jacob has no imagination. At first, Jacob will not have anything to do with the magical snowman. But he finally sneaks out and listens to the snowman. Ask students to tell why they think Jacob has a change of heart.

3 Peewee is a "peace lover." He thinks of others and wants people to be happy. Ask students to point out different things in the story that reveal Peewee's personality.

4 The kente cloth in this story represents a magical power. Have students write an original story in which some object has magical powers when held or worn. Allow time for students to share their stories with the class.

5 When the snowman tells his story to make Jacob proud of his African ancestors, he mentions many tribes. Have a pair of interested students research this and indicate these tribal areas on a map of Africa. (Mentioned are Timbuktu, Bornu, Zulu, Nuba, Bini, Ashanti, Tuareg, Zande.)

6 Africans and other groups use masks in ceremonies. If there is a shop in your town that sells masks, or a collector of masks, ask a resource person to visit the class and share and discuss African masks.

 ## *Brrr!*

FICTION

by James Stevenson
New York: Greenwillow Books, 1991. 32p. (unnumbered)

This picture book is illustrated in full color in a comic-book style and will appeal to primary-grade readers.

When the story begins, Mary Ann and Louie appear in front of Grandpa's house. They are sick of snow. Grandpa invites them to sit by the fire and hear his story of the winter of 1908, when it was *really* cold. Grandpa says it was so cold that sneezes froze, and the entire town was buried in snow. Grandpa and his brother, Wainey, called down chimneys trying to find their house that had disappeared in the snow.

Grandpa and Wainey went up a hill, slid down, and ran into a clothesline. They grabbed a sheet and were swept away in a gust of wind. They landed in a herd of deer. Then they made a giant snowman that fell over and turned into a giant snowball. It rolled right down Elm Street uncovering houses as it went.

So Wainey and Grandpa found their house, but it was covered in ice. Grandpa whispered something in Wainey's ear that made him give a loud cry that cracked the ice. Then they went inside.

When Mary Ann and Louie ask what Grandpa had whispered, he tells them he whispered, "I guess you'll never have ice cream again." At just this point, Uncle Wainey arrives at Grandpa's house and all four of them sit down by the fire to enjoy ice cream, which is good to eat on any kind of day.

Discussion Starters and Multidisciplinary Activities

1   Some of the words in this book are printed like ordinary text. Other words appear in "balloons" above the characters heads, the way dialogue usually appears in comics. Ask students whether they like this combined text approach.

2   Ask students whether they think that Grandpa, who was the older brother, took good care of his younger brother, Wainey. What events in the story support their opinions?

3   Wainey is too young to talk, he only cries and says, "Yump." Ask students if a baby they know uses some interesting "words" such as "yump." Discuss these words.

4   This story is a "tall tale." Cut sheets of typing paper in half and staple them into a cover to make blank books for students. The books will be roughly 4-1/4 inches wide and 11 inches tall. Give all students a blank "tall book" and ask them to write and illustrate an original tall tale. Allow time for students to share their books.

5   Many books give facts about world records. Have a pair of interested students, with the help of the media specialist, find out when and where the most snow fell and share this information with the class.

6   Ask students to estimate how long an ice cube takes to melt. Chart each student's guess on graph paper. Bring in two ice cubes. Put one in a sunny spot and the other out of the sun. Time the melting carefully. Did anyone guess correctly?

📖 *Dogteam*

FICTION

by Gary Paulsen

Illustrated by Ruth Wright Paulsen

New York: Delacorte Press, 1993. 32p. (unnumbered)

This picture book has minimal text and is illustrated with lovely watercolor paintings. It will appeal to primary-grade readers.

In this story, the dog racer harnesses his sled dogs in preparation to run at night. He chooses a night when there is a full moon, making it easy to see. The dogs tremble and make noises in their excitement at feeling their harnesses and knowing that they are about to run.

When the hook is freed from the snow, the dogs race off. The seven dogs race in and out of the trees, pulling the sled and rider behind them. They dash away from camps and people into the winter night. They leave the trees to race across a frozen lake, and then run back among the trees. Suddenly, they find they are not alone. Wolves join them briefly and then turn away into the darkness.

The dogs keep running until they finally see lights. They have made a big circle in the snow and have come home again.

The dogs are coated with ice and snow, and the snaps on their collars and harness will not open. But the dogs seem to be smiling with happiness because they love to race.

In the final picture, the dogs are howling at the sky as if they wanted this night and this run through the snow to last forever.

Discussion Starters and Multidisciplinary Activities

1. There is no conversation in this book. The man who rides in the sled does not speak to the dogs. Ask students to discuss why the author did not have the sled driver speak.

2. As soon as they realized they were getting into harness, these dogs began to tremble with excitement. Other pets get excited too. Someone's dog may dance up and down when it sees a leash and knows it is going for a walk. A cat may show excitement when his food dish is being filled. Ask students to share the way their pets respond to things.

3. Reread the page about the wolves. Ask students if they were frightened by the appearance of the wolves in the story. Why or why not?

4. The author and illustrator are connected with a famous sled dog race that is run every year, the Iditarod. Ask a pair of interested students to research this Alaska race and share with the class such information as when the race was first run, how long it is, and how fast it has been run.

5. Wolves have been a subject of controversy. They have been hunted and killed for raiding ranchers' stock. In some places, wolves have been reintroduced. Ask a pair of students to research this topic.

6. Many breeds of dogs are used in dogteams. Ask a pair of interested students to research different kinds of dogs that race in the Iditarod.

 *First Snow*

FICTION

by Kim Lewis

Cambridge, MA: Candlewick Press, 1993. 32p. (unnumbered)

This picture book will be enjoyed by kindergarten through second-grade students. The illustrations are soft, colored-pencil drawings depicting a rural setting.

When the story begins, Daddy is sick in bed. So Mommy, Sara, and Sara's teddy bear climb a hill with their dogs to take care of the sheep. It is cold and the wind is starting to blow. By the time they reach the lone pine tree at the top of the hill, the sky has turned white, and the first snow of the season begins. Their farm house appears to be a long way off.

Mommy hurries to feed the animals, and Sara helps. As they work, spreading hay out for the hungry sheep, the teddy bear drops and is accidentally left behind.

The snow begins to get thicker. As soon as the sheep are fed, Mommy and Sara hurry toward home.

Sara notices that Teddy is missing. Mommy explains that they cannot go back and look for him in the snow, but Sara sits down and does not want to go home without her precious bear. One of the sheep dogs comes up to them. The dog is carrying Teddy gently in his mouth.

Sara, Mommy, Teddy, and the dogs return to their home. They go inside and warm themselves by the fire. Then they give Daddy breakfast in bed. When Daddy asks who fed the sheep, Sara says that it was her, Mommy, and Teddy.

Discussion Starters and Multidisciplinary Activities

1   Ask students if they have climbed someplace high, and like Mommy in this story, felt that they were "on top of the world." Where were they, and what did it feel like?

2   Sara has a special toy, Teddy, that she takes with her everywhere. Have a teddy bear day at school. Each student may bring a teddy bear (or another favorite stuffed animal) to spend the day. Provide a time for sharing the bears.

3   Point out to students that the farm house and most of the fences in this story are made of stone. Ask them why the stone was used. Have they ever seen a stone house or stone fences? Where?

4   A dog is a hero in this story. It rescues the teddy bear. Ask an interested pair of students to research sheep dogs. What sorts of dogs are usually used for sheep herding? What characteristics do these dogs have? Do these dogs need special training? Have students report what they learn to the class.

5   Sheep are raised for a variety of purposes. One purpose is for the fine wool used in making garments. Try to locate someone in your community who spins and works with wool. Ask that person to visit your classroom and demonstrate carding and spinning wool.

6   There is a line, early in the book, which tell us that "the rooks are calling." Have a pair of students work with an adult volunteer to find out what rooks are and bring a picture and information about rooks to share with the class.

📖 *Geraldine's Big Snow*

FICTION

by Holly Keller

New York: Greenwillow Books, 1988. 24p. (unnumbered)

This picture book, with watercolor illustrations, will appeal to primary-grade students. There are approximately six to fifty words of text on each page.

The main character, Geraldine, is a pig. When the story begins, Geraldine is waiting for snow. Her sled and boots are by the door. She keeps looking out the window, waiting for the snow to begin. Her father heard a radio report that a big storm would be bringing a foot of snow.

Geraldine dresses warmly and goes out to wait for the snow. Outside, Geraldine meets a number of animals who are making preparations for the snow. Mrs. Wilson, a sheep, is bringing home a lot of apples because it will be hard to go shopping when it snows. Mr. Peters, a possum, is bringing home a lot of books to read. Mr. Harper, a fox, is putting out seeds for the birds who will get hungry when it snows. Uncle Albert is attaching a snowplow to his truck.

By supper time, there is still no snow. Geraldine falls asleep looking out the window at a star that is hiding behind a cloud. During the night, millions of snowflakes fall. When she awakens, the first sound Geraldine hears is Uncle Albert's snowplow.

On this lovely snowy day, Mrs. Wilson makes apple pies, Mr. Peters sits in front of the fireplace reading, Mr. Harper counts the birds at his feeder, and Geraldine goes sledding.

Discussion Starters and Multidisciplinary Activities

1 Ask students why they think Geraldine is so excited at the prospect of snow. Is this the first snow of the season? Has it been a long time since it has snowed? Or does Geraldine just love to go sledding whenever she can?

2 Each animal in the story gets ready for the snow and then enjoys favorite things when the snow finally arrives. Ask students what favorite things they enjoy doing on a snowy day.

3 Geraldine wonders if the weatherman could be wrong. Collect the forecasts for a week. Write down the predicted weather and high and lows. Record the actual data. Have students discuss whether the predictions were usually right or usually wrong.

4 The possum, Mr. Peters, has an unusual tail. In one of the pictures, it is wrapped around his rocking chair. With an adult volunteer or the help of a media specialist, have one or two students find out more about possums. What special uses does a possum have for its tail?

5 If possible, put a bird feeder outside your classroom window or at some other place on the school grounds where students can observe it? Build a simple feeder. Find out what kinds of seeds would be best for the birds in your area. Fill the feeder and observe. Remember, it may take several days for birds to begin to use your feeder.

6 There are many beautiful poems about snow. Read some of these. Then have students write original poems and place them on the classroom bulletin board.

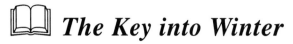 # *The Key into Winter*

FICTION

by Janet S. Anderson

Illustrated by David Soman

Morton Grove, IL: Albert Whitman, 1994. 28p. (unnumbered)

This picture book is illustrated with color drawings and will appeal to students in the primary grades.

Clara's family has an interesting custom. Four keys hang above the fireplace. As each season closes, the oldest woman in the family turns the key into the next season. Clara begs her Mama, Mattie, to tell her about the year when she was a little girl and tried to hide the key to keep winter from coming.

Mattie tells how the doctor said this would be grandmother's last autumn. Mattie begged her mother not to use the key into winter. Then autumn would stay and grandmother would not die.

On the last night of autumn, Mattie sneaked downstairs, and took the winter key. Mattie was sure that she had saved her grandmother. But the next day she learned about the problems she had caused. Mama put away the Christmas tree because there would be no winter this year. The sleds and ice skates have been packed away. Grandfather and father are in the barn saying that, because there is no winter, there will be no spring, summer, or harvest.

Grandmother was sad too. Without winter, she had no chance to see another spring. Mattie showed mother where she hid the key—out in the kitchen stove. The key was rescued, and that night, Grandmother turned the key. She lived to see another spring. As the story ends, Clara's grandmother prepares to tell her how *she* once almost lost the key into autumn.

Discussion Starters and Multidisciplinary Activities

1   This story tells about a beautiful family custom. It is carried out four times a year by the oldest woman in the family. Ask students if they have a special custom in their family that they would like to share with others.

2   Ask students to reflect on the seasons. Have them tell which season they would omit from the next year if one had to be left out. Ask students to explain why they selected this season.

3   When you have finished reading the story, ask students if they like the way it ends—suggesting that there is another story to hear, about a different key and a different season.

4   Working individually or in small groups, encourage students to write an original story modeled after this one. In their story, have grandmother tell Clara about how one of the keys to a season was almost lost.

5   Encourage students, in pairs, to play "Word Links" using seasonal words. One student writes a word, such as *snow*. The second student builds a new word, hooking it to the beginning or the end of snow. For example, the second student might write *wind* coming off of the *w* in snow, or *blizzards* coming down to end and connect with the *s* in snow.

6   Some people keep collections of old keys that they buy in antique shops. Invite a shop owner or a key collector to visit your class, show some old keys, and explain how they were used (for clocks, skates, doors, etc.).

 *Look! Snow!*

FICTION

by Kathryn O. Galbraith
Illustrated by Nina Montezinos
New York: Margaret K. McElderry Books, 1992. 32p. (unnumbered)

This picture book has only 21 words. The story is conveyed by the soft-colored, action-filled pictures. It will be enjoyed by kindergarten and first-grade readers.

The story begins in a classroom with a teacher and several pupils. The students are working at their desks. One points to the window where snowflakes are falling fast and says, "Look! Snow!"

In the next pictures, some students riding home from school with parents, and others are riding the school bus. The passengers are happily looking out the windows at the snow. At home, one of the children meets her father as he arrives from work. Children are shown looking out the house window as snow continues to fall during the night.

Pictures show children getting out of bed in the morning. They see a snowy world. In the next scenes, the teacher and pupils gather around the television or radio to listen to reports on which schools are closed. When the name "McCormick" is announced, the children are happy because it is a snow day, and there will be no school.

Everyone prepares to enjoy the day: skiing, making snow angels in the snow, and sledding. That night, the same girl goes to the window and cries, "Look! Snow!" It is snowing again.

Discussion Starters and Multidisciplinary Activities

1. If you live in an area where there are "snow days," students will quickly relate to the happy feeling of getting a day off from school. Ask students what they do for fun on these days.

2. Some people get their news from newspapers. Others rely on radio or television. Have students discuss how most people in their family keep up with the news.

3. Most students occasionally ride a bus, even if it is just on a special field trip. Ask the students to discuss what they like most and least about riding a school bus.

4. The bus driver is going to enjoy his day off, too. We see him ready to go skiing. Sometimes it is hard for students to realize that school personnel have a life away from school. It might be fun to have pairs of students interview school personnel asking them to name some hobby or sport they enjoy "off duty" and then share this information with the class.

5. Some of the children in this story made a snow-woman. Have students draw pictures of snow people or snow animals and then share them with the class. You might want to put their drawings on a class bulletin board.

6. The amount of moisture in a snowfall can be surprisingly low. If you live where it snows, try this class experiment. Put out a clean coffee can to catch the snow. Bring the can inside and measure the depth of the snow. Cover the can (to prevent evaporation) and let the snow melt. Measure the amount of water. How do the two compare?

📖 *Out on the Ice in the Middle of the Bay*

FICTION

by Peter Cumming
Illustrated by Alice Priestley
Toronto: Annick Press, 1993. 32p. (unnumbered)

This picture book, set in the Arctic, contains soft, full-color illustrations, and will be enjoyed by primary-grade readers.

When the story opens, young Leah is at home with her father. He warns her not to go out because polar bears are nearby. But when father falls asleep, Leah pulls on her warm parka and creeps outside. She sees a big iceberg out in the bay.

On the far side of the iceberg, a mother polar bear is feeding her cub, Nanook. The bear warns her cub not to stray away because there are humans nearby. After the mother bear falls asleep, Nanook wanders off.

Leah wanders out on the ice toward the iceberg while Nanook walks farther away from his mother. When Leah's father awakens, he grabs his gun and goes out looking for his daughter. Nanook's mother awakens and begins to run after her cub.

Out on the ice, Leah and Nanook meet. Leah curls up near the furry bear. Nanook nuzzles her. When Leah's father meets Nanook's mother, the bear swings at Leah's father and misses. Father shoots at the bear and misses. The explosion of the gun makes Leah and Nanook sit up. Leah runs to her father and Nanook runs to his mother. Slowly the bears and the people back away from each other. Snowmobiles come, and Leah, warm and happy, goes home, while the bears remain in the middle of the bay.

Discussion Starters and Multidisciplinary Activities

1. Ask students why Leah went outside after her father had told her to stay inside. Was Leah looking for polar bears or was she up to something else?

2. Ask students to discuss how Leah and Nanook were similar and how Leah's father and Nanook's mother were similar.

3. Leah and her father backed away from the bears. The bears backed away from the people. Ask students what they think might have happened if either set had run away from the other.

4. Polar bears have special features to help them survive. Ask a pair of interested students to research polar bears, with the help of a media specialist. How tall does a polar bear stand? How heavy is a full-grown mother bear? How big are baby polar bears when they are born? Have the students share their information with the class.

5. The author expresses his thanks, in the book's front matter, to the Arctic Awareness Program for his opportunity to travel and write on Ellesmere Island. Have an interested pair of students locate Ellesmere Island on a map and show the other members of the class where it is.

6. Eskimos wear special clothing to keep warm. Ask interested students to research and find pictures of parkas, boots, and leggings that are worn. These may be photocopied from books or magazines. Bring these in to share with the rest of the class.

 *Snow Company*

FICTION

by Marc Harshman
Illustrated by Leslie W. Bowman
New York: Cobblehill Books, 1990. 32p. (unnumbered)

This is a picture book with color illustrations and much text. It will be enjoyed by students in grades two through four.

The story opens with two boys coming home early from school in a blizzard. Ronnie wants to throw snowballs, but his brother, Teddy, is eager to get inside where it is warm. He knows that his Mom does not want Ronnie to become sick again.

The boys do chores around the house and wonder if there'll be school tomorrow. Then they enjoy hot chocolate. Teddy reads a book while Ronnie takes a rest.

The snow storm is the worst in 20 years. Jim's truck goes into a ditch, and he comes to wait in the house. More people get stuck. Mrs. Hart arrives and so does Mrs. Mason and her baby. All these new visitors come inside and join Teddy's family for dinner. Dad calls to say that he is stuck in town.

It turns into quite a party. Mrs. Hart tells stories about when Teddy's dad was a little boy in her class. She guesses all of Ronnie's riddles and tells new ones. Jim tells stories about hiking all over this area long ago.

The electricity goes out, and Teddy thinks that's great. Young Mrs. Mason tells stories that her grandparents told her about the farm. That night, people bed down on couches and on the floor under warm covers. Teddy reflects that the next time company comes, he will have quite a story to tell.

Discussion Starters and Multidisciplinary Activities

1 Although there are two boys in this story, Ronnie and Teddy, Teddy is the main character. Ask students how they know which boy is the main character.

2 Although the people who come to spend the night all know each other, they are not close friends. Ask the students whether or not they think these people will maintain these new friendships after the blizzard. Why or why not?

3 If all these visitors dropped in during a blizzard to have dinner and spent the night, and students had to choose between Jim, Mrs. Hart, or Mrs. Mason and her baby, who would they choose, and why?

4 Many students enjoy riddles like the one told in this book. You might want to set aside a riddle hour in class. Ahead of time, ask each child to find a riddle to share. During the riddle hour, let students try to "stump" one another.

5 We know that Teddy's dad was stuck in town and spent the night with Grandma Price. Have students write an original story in which they describe what happened to Dad and Grandma Price during the blizzard. Allow time for students to share their stories.

6 Students might enjoy this project: take a sheet of 12-by-18-inch art paper and divide it in half. On the left, draw and show a scene before the snow, and on the right, show the same scene after a snow storm. The scene might be in the city or country, with or without people and animals.

From *Rainy, Windy, Snowy, Sunny Days*. © 1996. Teacher Ideas Press. (800) 237-6124.

Snow Toward Evening: A Year in a River Valley: Nature Poems

FICTION

Selected by Josette Frank
Illustrations by Thomas Locker
New York: Dial Press, 1990. 32p. (unnumbered)

This book contains a poem for each month of the year, plus one to greet the new year, by 13 different poets. The illustrations are reproductions of paintings done by landscape painter Thomas Locker in his studio in the Hudson River valley.

The title poem, which this book is included here, is "Snow Toward Evening" by Melville Cane. The accompanying illustration shows a snowscape with trees and rocks just as the sun is setting.

The poem describes how the sky turns grey and the bitter cold day becomes still. The snow comes with dusk like millions of petals from some invisible blossoming tree. The poem is written in 10 lines and uses end rhymes in a variable pattern.

Other poems and poets included are: "January" by John Updike; "When Skies Are Low and Days Are Dark" by N. M. Bodecker; "Mountain Brook" by Elizabeth Coatsworth; "In Time of Silver Rain" by Langston Hughes; "Daffodils" by William Wordsworth; "Afternoon on a Hill" by Edna St. Vincent Millay; "The River" by Charlotte Zolotow; "Something Told the Wild Geese" by Rachel Field; "Mountain Wind" by Barbara Kunz Loots; "Wind Has Shaken Autumn Down" by Tony Johnston; "Fly Away" by Christina Rossetti; and "A New Year" by Mary Carolyn Davies.

Discussion Starters and Multidisciplinary Activities

1   Show students the shape of this 10-line poem. Ask them why they think the poet included only one word in line five?

2   In the first stanza, the words *still* and *chill* come at the end of two adjacent lines. In the second stanza, the lines ending in *white* and *night* are separated by two other lines. Ask students what effects are achieved by having rhymes close together or separated?

3   Ask students to invent another name for this poem.

4   Ask students to study the lovely painting that illustrates "Snow Toward Evening." It is a country scene with trees, rocks, shrubs and hills. But snow also falls on small towns, big cities, and school yards. Ask students to create their own chalk drawing of snow beginning to fall at dusk. Share the drawings on a bulletin board.

5   Students are interested in world records. Using reference books, ask a few interested students to find interesting records about snow and cold. What is the record snowfall? When and where did it occur? What is the coldest recorded temperature in the United States?

6   The subject "snow" is also mentioned in another poem included in this book, "Wind Has Shaken Autumn Down." Read other snow poems to the students. Ask them to write original poems which could be serious or funny, rhymed or unrhymed. Display the results on your class bulletin board.

📖 *When the Mountain Sings*

by John MacLean
Boston: Houghton Mifflin, 1992. 168p.

FICTION

This chapter book revolves around a boy's introduction to championship slalom racing. It will be of interest to fourth- and fifth-grade readers. It is told in the first person from the viewpoint of thirteen-year-old Sam.

Sam can remember his first ski lesson. His mentor and coach, Phil, tells Sam that he is now ready to race. But Sam is unsure of himself.

In the early, cold hours of the morning, as he is riding with his coach and other young skiers to a competition, Sam thinks how nice it would be at home, snug in bed. For the most part, he likes the kids he skis with: Leah and Molly, the two girls on the team; and Louie, Duncan, Josh, and Felix.

Once Sam begins to race, he quickly sets his sights on making it into the top 40, so that he would be eligible to ski in the championships. He is disappointed when he is named as an alternate for the championship. Three boys who do qualify are injured, thereby giving Sam a spot in the races.

Sam races and proves to be the best thirteen-year-old on the mountain that day. He comes to understand the rhythm of the mountains. He gives his trophy to Felix in the hospital, and realizes that winning does not change everything.

Discussion Starters and Multidisciplinary Activities

1 The coach, Phil, is described through his actions. Ask students if they think that Phil is a good coach or if they would change the way he acts. Why do they feel as they do?

2 Sam and his brother, Bo, are supportive, rather than competitive. Ask students to point out action in the story that shows how the brothers relate to one another.

3 Sam gave his trophy away to his friend, Felix. Ask readers if that surprised them or if they had expected this. Why?

4 Elementary students often like to make a special reading spot someplace in the room. During this study of snow and ice, they might enjoy creating a reading igloo. Well in advance, they will need to collect empty plastic gallon milk jugs. Enough of these, taped together, will make a fine reading igloo.

5 The book jacket points out that Olympic hopefuls begin in the USAA race program. Have a pair of students find out more about the USAA race program. How is it organized? Where do races take place? What age groups are involved?

6 Ask a pair of students to research the Olympic Winter Games. Where and when will they next be held? What events are included? For a few of the race events, ask the students to graph the results of gold, silver, and bronze medalists with flags from the countries that the winners represented. Does this reveal one or a few countries dominate in a specific area?

◆ *Bridges* ◆

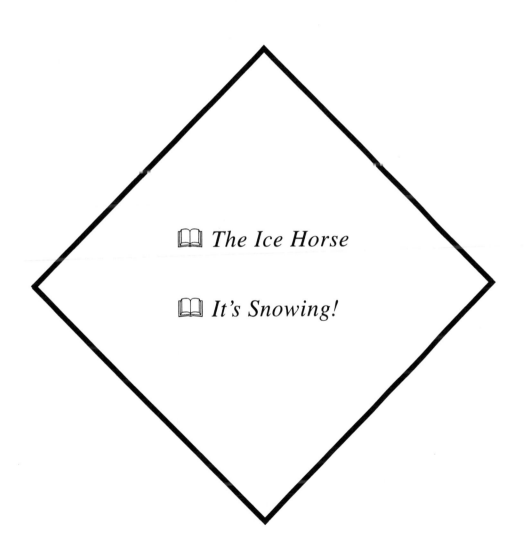

📖 *The Ice Horse*

📖 *It's Snowing!*

 # *The Ice Horse*

BRIDGES

by Candace Christiansen
Illustrated by Thomas Locker
New York: Dial Books, 1993. 32p. (unnumbered)

This picture book is illustrated with full-color paintings and will be of interest to students in grades two through four. The story explains ice harvesting on the Hudson River.

In November, people along the Hudson River get ready for the ice harvest. Uncle Joe arrives on a steamboat with his horse, Max. Uncle Joe asks Jack to take the horse to the barn. Jack is twelve, and proud to be able to help this year.

For the next several days after school, Jack helps Uncle Joe sharpen his ice saws. By the end of the week, the ice is ready. The horse is fitted with spiked horseshoes and Uncle Joe explains what to do if the horse should fall in the water. With a special tool, they mark the ice into blocks. They cut a channel across the river and push the blocks of ice through the channel. Conveyor belts carry the ice to the icehouse.

Uncle Joe spends some of his time in the icehouse. Meanwhile, Jack and Max have become a team. One afternoon, they get too close to the edge of the channel and Max falls into the water. Jack pulls the rope the way his uncle showed him. Uncle Joe and other men come and begin to haul Max out. Max is all right.

When the ice harvest is over, Uncle Joe prepares to return to the city. Jack gets to stay with him during spring vacation to deliver ice in the city. Next winter, Jack will work in the ice harvest again.

Possible Topics for Further Student Investigation

1. This bridge book gives a good deal of information about the way in which ice was harvested from the Hudson River for use in New York City. Ask a pair of interested students to further research this topic, with the help of a media specialist. Where was the ice stored? How was it transported to the city? How was the ice delivered from door to door? When were iceboxes replaced with refrigerators? Have the students share what they learn with the class.

2. If you live where it gets cold, you can perform this experiment outdoors for your class: Punch three holes equally spaced around the top of three one-pound coffee cans. Put string through the holes and knot the strings to form loops for hanging the cans. In the bottom of each can, punch one hole. Make one hole with a thumbtack. Make a slightly larger hole with a nail in another can, and a still bigger hole in the third can. Fill three empty jars with water. Tint each with a different food coloring. On a cold morning, hang the coffee cans outdoors in a safe place on the school grounds and fill each with one color of water. Soon you will have colorful icicles to share. Predict which icicles will be longest. Why?

3. There are many kinds of horses, and different breeds are used for different purposes. Ask a pair of students interested in horses to do some research. What breeds might be used as ice horses? What breeds are used for other work purposes? Have students share their information with the class.

 *It's Snowing!*

BRIDGES

by Margaret Cosgrove
New York: Dodd, Mead, 1980. 48p.

This book is two-thirds text with one-third simple, black, blue, and white illustrations. It will appeal to students in grades three and four.

This bridge book contains elements of fiction and elements of nonfiction. It begins by describing a winter snowstorm as a cloak of white dropped by a sky giant. Everything is covered in some sort of white garment, but there is no need for zippers or buttons, because these are simply coats of snow.

The next section explains how snow is made. Water vapor droplets attach themselves to a tiny speck of dust or ice and form a single snow crystal. The color of snow and the way that it muffles noises is discussed. The text explains that snow may fall in a small area or more than several states as it sweeps on its way. Storms may move slowly or swiftly.

There is also a section on different words Eskimos use for snow, such as *annui*, *upsik*, *gali*, and *theh-ni-zee*. Information is provided on avalanches, rescue dogs, glaciers, blizzards, frostbite, and snow-blindness. Text and pictures explain how some parts of plants and how some animals live beneath the snow. Also discussed is how snow can be a hardship to animals and birds. The book concludes with a list of safety dos and don'ts.

Possible Topics for Further Student Investigation

1. Depending on where you live, there may be an Eskimo arts shop nearby, or someone who has collected Eskimo artifacts. Ask such a person to visit the class and bring in items to share. These items might include carvings of bears or seals, fur garments, jewelry, bone sunglasses, masks, hunting knives, fish snares, and photographs.

2. Many parts of the country have search-and-rescue dog units. These dogs are used to hunt for people caught in avalanches, but they are also used in disaster areas where people have been caught in collapsed buildings or in the woods for rescuing people who have become lost. If such a unit is in your area, ask if one of the dog handlers (and dog) can visit your classroom and discuss the work of search-and-rescue dogs. What dogs work well for these purposes? What sort of training is required?

3. This book mentions that the snowshoe hare turns from brown to white in winter as a sort of camouflage, so that it blends in with its surroundings. Ask a small group of interested students to research this topic. What other birds or animals that live in snowy regions change their feather or fur color during the winter? Try to find pictures of these birds and animals in both their winter and summer colors. Bring the pictures and any other information learned on this topic to share with others in the class.

Snowy Days

 Nonfiction Connections

📖 _Glaciers_

📖 _High in the Wind: The Snow Geese_

📖 _The Ice Ages_

📖 _Ice Skating Is for Me_

📖 _Icebergs, Titans of the Oceans_

📖 _Icebergs and Glaciers_

📖 _Snow_

📖 _Snow and Ice_

📖 _Snow Is Falling_

📖 _Snow Sports_

📖 _Weather & Climate_

📖 _Winter Weather_

 *Glaciers*

by Michael George

Mankato, MN: Creative Education, 1991. 40p.

Creative Education has published a series of books—*Stars, Glaciers, the Sun, Volcanoes*—which are photographic essays. This book has dramatic, full-color photographs and will appeal to students in grades three through five.

This book defines glaciers as thick, flowing rivers of ice, which, over millions of years, sculpt the earth. Glaciers are born in cold climates where there is snow. In some areas, temperatures never rise high enough to melt the snow. The fresh snow piles up, year after year. In time, the tremendous weight fuses the snow together and forces out pockets of air. The snow becomes a slab of hard, blue ice.

When the slab becomes large enough, gravity pulls the slab down the mountain on which it has been resting. Once the ice begins to move, it is called a glacier. A glacier follows the path of existing mountains. A glacier's speed depends upon the thickness of the slab, the steepness of the slope, and the temperature. The middle of a glacier moves faster than its edges, and the surface of a glacier moves faster than its deeper layers.

The glacier carves a U-shaped trough. The material it carves away as it moves is dumped at the glacier's base and is called a terminal moraine. Warm weather may stop the forward flow of a glacier or cause it to retreat. When a glacier reaches the sea, ice shelves extend over the water. Waves smash these shelves, breaking off floating chunks of ice, called icebergs.

Possible Topics for Further Student Investigation

1 Alaska is well known for its many spectacular glaciers. Ask a pair of students, with the help of a local travel agency, to gather brochures and information about places in Alaska where glaciers can be observed. Ask these students to plan such a trip and then give a "travelogue" to their classmates explaining where they would go and what they would see on a trip from their town to some of Alaska's great glaciers and then home again. Show travel brochures or other available pictures of the sights.

2 Some scientists argue that another ice age is overdue. Others maintain that global warming is raising the temperature of our planet and that we are in danger of having great sheets of ice melt and flood much of earth's coastal land. Ask six interested students (three for each opinion) to gather information on these two possibilities and present their data to the class in the form of an oral debate. Students on both sides should cite the sources of information for their predictions.

3 Icebergs have caused a number of wrecks at sea. Of these, perhaps the most famous is the sinking of the passenger liner *Titanic*. Ask a pair of interested students to do some research on the sinking of the Titanic. When did it sink? How many lives were lost and how many saved? Was human error involved? Ask these students to prepare a written report on this topic, citing their sources of information.

High in the Wind: The Snow Geese

NONFICTION CONNECTIONS

by Lynn M. Stone
Vero Beach, FL: Rourke, 1991. 48p.

This is an easy-to-read book illustrated with color photographs. It is part of the Animal Odysseys series.

The book begins with a puzzle. Where are the nesting grounds of the snow goose? Ornithologists knew that they must breed somewhere in the remote north, but were not able to pinpoint the nesting grounds on the Arctic plains of northern Canada until early in the twentieth century. It was not until the 1960s that ornithologists discovered that "blue geese" were simply a color variation, or phase, of the all-white snow geese.

The largest number of snow geese, more than 400,000, winter in California's Central Valley. Other flocks have been seen along Puget Sound, Washington, and in New Mexico, Nevada, and Mexico. The U.S. Fish and Wildlife Service manages much of the winter range of the snow geese.

The author explains the reasons why birds migrate, and how they orient themselves using the sun and the position of the stars as references.

One section of the book is devoted to a discussion of the meadow of mosses, lichens, grasses, and tiny flowers that make up the Arctic tundra. Another section discusses the predators, including the Arctic fox and gulls, which attack snow goose eggs and goslings. A map is included, which shows the primary migration routes for snow geese in North America.

Possible Topics for Further Student Investigation

1 If your students enjoyed reading about migrating geese, they might find other migrations interesting. Another animal that makes an interesting migration is the northern elephant seal. Ask a pair of students to locate books or magazine articles on this animal. Their research on the topic should include at least three sources of information. Using their notes, these students can make an oral presentation to the class.

2 An interesting bird that undergoes a color change at the approach of winter is the ptarmigan. Ask an interested pair of students to find pictures of this bird taken at various times of the year in its natural setting, or make a series of color drawings, using a medium of their choice, to illustrate the changes in coloring. Label each and post these on the classroom bulletin board.

3 Nonfiction writers do a lot of research to produce a picture book. Ask an interested pair of students to write and illustrate a children's picture book about a snow goose. It can be any length, although a typical picture book is often 32 pages. They should research and gather information until they are able to tell the story of a gosling, born in the Arctic, surviving the attacks of various predators, feeding and growing during the summer days, and then making its first migration south. Students should illustrate their book and share it with a kindergarten or first-grade class.

The Ice Ages

by Roy A. Gallant
New York: Franklin Watts, 1985. 64p.

This book is part of a series of books published by Franklin Watts called First Books. This book is mostly text and is illustrated with black-and-white photographs. It will be of interest to students in grades three through five. The book is divided into eight chapters and contains a glossary and index.

This book begins with a discussion of the Little Ice Age that gripped Europe from about 1400 to 1850. During this time, there was a gradual lowering of temperature by a few degrees, with longer winters and shorter summers. Growing seasons were significantly shortened. Several glaciers in the Alps advanced far enough to crush houses.

Chapter two discusses the various ice ages that have gripped our planet. Over the past 700,000 years, climatologists say that there have been seven known glacial periods. Between each was a period of warming known as an interglacial period, such as the present period. Currently, it is warmer than it has been for more than 90 percent of the past 1 million years.

Chapters three and four detail the advance of glaciers and the tracking of the great ice. Chapter five tells about ice age animals and the game hunters of about 11,000 years ago.

Final chapters discuss why ice ages come and go, how we can date events in the earth's past, and visiting mountain glaciers in America's National Parks.

Possible Topics for Further Student Investigation

1   Have pairs of interested students write to Glacier National Park, Mount McKinley National Park, Mount Rainier National Park, Olympic National Park, and Yosemite National Park. The students should explain in their letters that they are studying about glaciers and request any available park pamphlets. The students should be reminded to enclose with their letters a self-addressed, stamped 9-by-12-inch envelope for the park information center's reply. Materials received should be shared with the class.

2   One of the most interesting of the extinct animals that lived during the Ice Age was the saber-toothed cat. Ask a pair of interested students to research this topic. When and where did this animal live? How big was it? What fossil records have been found? Ask the students to prepare a presentation for the class on their topic, including drawings showing how the saber-toothed cat looked.

3   A small group of students might find it an interesting challenge to write a play script in that tells the story of villagers living in Europe during the Little Ice Age. In the dialogue, the villagers could describe the changes that they noticed taking place in the seasons, crops, and so on. They could be worried about the gradual approach of an enormous glacier, which they fear will destroy their homes. When the group is ready, have the students present their short play for the enjoyment of the rest of the class.

📖 *Ice Skating Is for Me*

by Lowell A. Dickmeyer and Lin Rolens
Photographs by Alan Oddie
Minneapolis: Lerner, 1980. 48p.

NONFICTION CONNECTIONS

This book is approximately half text and half black-and-white photographs of young skaters. It was prepared under the supervision of the former president of the Ice Skating Institute of America.

This book begins with a girl and boy, Heather and Lewis, who try ice skating for the first time. The size of skates, sharpness of blades, and other information is given. The authors explain that most people fall when they begin skating, but falling on the ice is different from falling on pavement because you slide and are less likely to hurt yourself.

The instructor in the book explains how to keep knees bent and back straight and to lean forward a little to try to find a comfortable balance on skates. Gradu-ally, standing near the rail, Heather and Lewis begin to stand and then glide on ice.

Since their first experience is successful, the two students begin to take skating classes. The book shows detailed pictures of figure skates, hockey skates without toe picks, and speed skates that have long blades. There is also information about the bottom of each skate blade and its edges.

Their new skating instructor, Jill, shows Heather and Lewis how to fall and get up again, and introduces other techniques such as stroking, push offs, snowplow stops, and the backward swizzle. She explains some of the badges that skaters earn.

Possible Topics for Further Student Investigation

1. Students who choose to read this book will probably be those who have participated in ice skating or are interested in trying it. Some schools schedule small-group activity days when students can devote an afternoon to work with an adult in an area of interest, such as painting, acting, science experiments, and so on. If possible, and if there is an ice skating rink in your area, arrange for a small group of students to ice skate. Parental permission and arrangements for rental of skates, instruction, and so on will be necessary. The small groups of students may want to share their experiences with the class.

2. If Winter Olympic Games are taking place or soon scheduled, there will be many students who watch parts of the games on television. Ice skating, in its various forms, is a popular spectator sport. Interested students may want to choose one or more ice skating events and trace the history of gold, silver, and bronze Olympic Champions in these events. They could prepare a chart listing the year, the medal winners, and the countries which they represented in the games.

3. Students may note when reading this book that styles in skating costumes, like other clothes, change over the years. A pair of interested students may want to photocopy pictures from magazines and books of skating champions from different years and post them, with dates of the photos, on a class bulletin board to point out how both the costumes of men and women have changed.

📖 *Icebergs, Titans of the Oceans*

NONFICTION CONNECTIONS

by Jenny Wood

Milwaukee: Gareth Stevens Children's Books, 1991. 32p.

This book is part of the four-volume Wonderworks of Nature series. It has simple text and is illustrated with color photographs and drawings. It will be enjoyed by primary-grade students.

This book begins by explaining what an iceberg is: a chunk of ice that breaks off as a glacier reaches the sea; or a piece that cracks and breaks off from an ice sheet, becoming an iceberg. Icebergs float because as water freezes, it expands. So a volume of ice is lighter than an equal volume of liquid water. Icebergs look white instead of clear because of tiny gas bubbles trapped in the ice, or because they are covered with snow. Icebergs come in all shapes and sizes.

Icebergs sometimes float into shipping lanes and can be a hazard. An International Ice Patrol keeps track of the movement of icebergs in the Atlantic.

A section of the book is devoted to creatures that live in the polar lands: polar bears, walruses, and seals in the Arctic; and penguins and seals in the Antarctic.

Another section explains that icebreakers are ships designed to travel through ice-covered waters and are used to rescue ships trapped in the ice, as well as to escort supply ships and carry out scientific research.

The book concludes with an exciting story of three whales trapped in the ice and how two were rescued.

Possible Topics for Further Student Investigation

1. When we think of birds, we think of flying, but penguins are birds that cannot fly. Ask a group of students to research the penguins of the Antarctic region. Each student might choose one of the seven species that live there, draw a picture of the penguin being researched, and find out other information such as: its size, what it eats, how the chicks are raised, and so on. The group should share their findings with the class and put their labeled drawings on a class bulletin board.

2. There are a number of different kinds of seals. Ask a few interested students to research this topic. What different kinds of seals are there? Where do they live? How do they raise their pups? What poses the greatest danger to seals? How long can they stay under water before coming up to breathe? Are there laws protecting seals from being killed for their fur? These students should give an oral report to the class sharing the information that they have learned.

3. Students might make some predictions and then carry out experiments with ice cubes to determine whether their predictions are right or wrong. Would adding sugar or salt to water cause it to freeze faster or slower than ordinary tap water? Does water freeze into ice cubes faster or slower than soda pop? Using an ice cube tray, can students demonstrate that water expands when it freezes? After experimenting, have students share their data and observations with the class.

📖 *Icebergs and Glaciers*

by Seymour Simon
New York: William Morrow, 1987. 32p. (unnumbered)

This is a large-format book with a clear, simple text that is illustrated with full-page color photographs. It will be enjoyed by readers in grades three and four.

This book begins by explaining that in some parts of the world the upper slopes and peaks of high mountains are places of everlasting snow, above the snow line. These are the places where glaciers are born. Countless snowflakes falling in these areas first clump together, trapping air bubbles inside. The weight of more snow pushes out the air until, gradually, the snow turns to blue, airless ice. These ice crystals pack together into thick, heavy fields of ice.

When the mass of ice begins to move by sliding over the ground, perhaps a few inches a year or even many feet a day, it has become a glacier. Sometimes the glacier creeps forward, and at other times it slides on meltwater.

In the past and in the present, scientists have studied glaciers and their movements. Factors involved in the movement of glaciers are the thickness of ice, the steepness of the slope, and temperature, which causes meltwater under the glacier.

There is discussion of crevasses, moraines, ice caps, the Antarctic ice sheets, icebergs, the International Ice Patrol, possible uses for icebergs in the future, and the Pleistocene Ice Ages.

Possible Topics for Further Student Investigation

1. One of the scientists mentioned in this book is a Swiss naturalist named Louis Agassiz. He studied various aspects of glaciers. Have a pair of interested students find out more about Agassiz. When and where did he live? Where did he go to study glaciers? What were some of his most significant findings? What other scientists are famous for their work with glaciers? Ask these students to share what they learn with the class.

2. One of the photographs in this book shows a scientist using an instrument called a transit to study the movement of a glacier. Students may have seen engineers using one of these instruments during highway construction. Is there someone in your community who has a transit and is familiar with its use? If so, ask this resource person to bring a transit to your class. The resource person can explain what a transit is, how it works, and for what purposes it is used.

3. It is hard for students (and adults) to grasp information when large periods of time are involved. Sometimes a pictorial representation helps. Ask a small group of interested students to prepare a time line of prehistoric times and mount it somewhere in the classroom. During the Pleistocene, they should indicate the various ice ages. On a map of the world beneath the time line, these students can show which portions of Canada, the United States, Britain, Russia, Germany, Poland, Austria, Italy, and France were covered with sheets of ice.

📖 *Snow*

by John Bianchi and Frank B. Edwards
Ontario: Bungalo Books, 1992. 49p.

Snow is part of a series of children's books, Learning for the Fun of It. Published in Canada as a Bungalo Book, *Snow* is copublished in the United States by Firefly books. The colorful artwork in the book is humorous and entertaining, and will appeal to third- through fifth-graders.

The book begins with a discussion of sublimation—the chain reaction that takes place when water vapor in a cloud becomes "super cool" and bumps into tiny dust particles, changing them into ice crystals. There are interesting facts about snowflakes and simple drawings illustrating the different shapes of crystals.

The section on glaciers and icebergs contains some facts that will be fascinating to young readers. This is followed by a discussion of various ice ages, changes in world climate, and famous storms and blizzards.

This is followed by information about ways of travelling over snow, including snowshoes, skis, sleds, snowmobiles, toboggans, and the use of sled dogs.

A section on the ways that cities remove snow is balanced by a section on having fun in the snow, which includes everything from snowballs to skis.

The ways people adapt to cold, and the various animals that live in snowy lands and the kinds of tracks they leave concludes the book.

Possible Topics for Further Student Investigation

1   An interesting section in this book discusses animal tracks left in the snow. Of course tracks can also be left in sand and dirt. Ask a small group of students to research animal tracks using books or magazine articles that include drawings or photographs of animals and of the tracks they leave. Make photocopies of both animals and tracks, number them, and put them on a bulletin board. See if classmates can match the pictures of various animals to the numbers identifying the animals that made the tracks.

2   Students probably already know how to fold paper and use scissors to cut snowflake shapes. Taking this one step further leads to an interesting art project. Cut snowflakes from squares of white paper that are three different sizes. Paste the largest snowflake near the bottom of a sheet of blue paper. Paste a middle-sized snowflake on top of the first. These two form the body of a snowman. Put the smallest snowflake on top to be the head. Then decorate your snow person using bits of colored paper. You might cut a fringed red scarf, add a hat and stick arms, or even an orange, carrot-shaped nose.

3   A snowshoe looks like an enormous paw made of leather lacing on a hardwood frame. It spreads a person's weight over a large enough area to prevent sinking in the snow. Find someone in your community who has a pair of snowshoes. Ask that person to visit your class and explain how snowshoes are worn and used. Be sure to follow up with a thank-you letter expressing your appreciation.

Snow and Ice

NONFICTION CONNECTIONS

by Joy Palmer
Austin, TX: Raintree Steck-Vaughn, 1993. 32p.

This book is part of the First Start Series on general science topics for children. It presents information on snow and ice simply and clearly using photos and art. The print is large and the text is easy for primary-grade students to read.

The book begins with an explanation of how droplets of water freeze, change into ice crystals, and when they are large enough, fall as snowflakes. There is a pictorial representation of the water cycle.

Brief sections are presented on hailstones, frost, and icicles. The effects of freezing and thawing are shown. A vocabulary of snow-related words is presented in context throughout the book including such words as *blizzards*, *drifts*, *snowplows*, *glaciers*, and *avalanches*.

A section is devoted to a discussion of the polar lands and how people travel and survive the harsh weather in these regions.

Photographs and drawings present some of the plants, trees, birds, and animals that live in snowy regions. Included are some that migrate and hibernate.

There is also a brief chapter on many of the activities that can be enjoyed in the snow such as skiing, making snow figures, and playing ice hockey.

The book concludes with a glossary of terms and some suggestions on things students might like to do.

Possible Topics for Further Student Investigation

1 If you live in a snowy place, here is a simple science experiment that allows students to find out how much water is in snow. Take a large, empty coffee can and set it outside where it can fill up with snow. Carry it gently inside and push a thin dowel into the snow to the bottom of the can. Be careful not to shake or bang the can. Mark the spot on the dowel that shows the depth of the snow. Measure this length carefully. Put a lid on the can of snow and allow it to melt at room temperature. Using your dowel, measure the depth of the water. You will find that several inches of snow will melt into only a few inches of water.

2 You might enjoy writing snow poems. An acrostic poem spells out the name of the subject by the first letters of the poem. Possible topics might be icicles, mittens, sledding, and so on. For example:

S itting outside in the cold,
N ot far from my back door
O nly two days old,
W earing my bright red scarf
M ittenless, with rock buttons,
A nd an orange carrot for a nose
N ot looking forward to a sunny afternoon.

3 There have been many famous explorers of the Arctic and Antarctic. Ask a pair of students to research one of these explorers and present an oral report to the class. Possible names to consider are: Robert Edwin Peary, Roald Amundsen, Captain C. J. Phipps, Captain Bob Bartlett, Frederick A. Cook, Richard E. Byrd, Sir Ernest Shackleton, Commander R. F. Scott, and Jean B. Charcot.

Snow Is Falling

by Franklyn M. Branley
Illustrated by Holly Keller
New York: Thomas Y. Crowell, 1986. 32p.

This picture book is part of the series Let's-Read-and-Find-Out Science Books. Suitable for the primary grades, with short, easy to read sentences and simple vocabulary, this book has colorful illustrations.

As the book opens, a young girl and her father are walking the dog at night. Snow is falling, may fall all night and all day, until it is very deep and covers lawns and roofs.

Drawings indicate what a snowflake might look like through a magnifying glass. Although each one is different, every snowflake will have six sides. It will always be cold when snow falls, cold enough that water vapor freezes in the air and makes snowflakes.

Dry and wet snow are discussed along with many things that children might enjoy doing in the snow such as skiing, sledding, or building a snowman.

The book explores whether or not snow is helpful to plants, animals, and people. Snow covers plants like a blanket and protects them from wind, ice, and cold. Snow also helps keep it warmer for animals that live in underground burrows. Melted snow provides people with water, from wells, streams, and rivers.

The problems of snow are also shown, including blizzards that cause cars to get stuck and that blow down power lines, as well as sudden spring melting that may cause flooding.

Possible Topics for Further Student Investigation

1. This book suggests a simple science experiment that students may wish to try. Hang one thermometer outdoors from a tree on a snowy day. Bury another thermometer in the snow. After waiting one hour, read the temperature from each thermometer. You should find that the thermometer buried in the snow showed a warmer temperature than the thermometer exposed to air.

2. One of the hazards of snow is that it sometimes prevents birds from finding sufficient food to live. As a class project, you might decide to make bird feeders. One way to do this is to gather enough pine cones so that everyone in the class can have one. Take a sturdy string and tie it in a loop tightly to the pine cone so that it can easily be hung from a tree. Among the scales of the pine cone, press pieces of ground suet.

3. Read some poems about snow such as "A Patch of Old Snow" by Robert Frost or "Snow Party" by Aileen Fisher. Choose enough examples so that students recognize poems can be long or short, funny or serious, rhymed or unrhymed. Discuss how compact language makes a poem different from a story. Brainstorm some ideas related to snow that might make good topics for a poem: a snowman, going skiing, sledding down a hill, dressing up in warm clothes, freezing toes, a snowball fight, making a snow dragon, and so on. Have everyone write and illustrate an original snow poem. Display the poems on a class bulletin board.

📖 *Snow Sports*

by Norman Barrett
New York: Franklin Watts, 1987. 32p.

This book is part of the Picture Library Series of visual reference books. The text is simple and the book is generously illustrated with drawings and color photographs. It will be enjoyed by students in grades two through four.

This book contains brief sections on skiing, downhill racing, slalom, freestyle, cross-country, ski jumping, and other snow sports. It also includes some facts and records as well as a glossary and index.

The book opens with a drawing of a ski jump, showing the various positions of the jumper, from takeoff to landing, and ways that competitors are judged for style, control, and accuracy.

The book includes beginning skiers as well as competitive racers. Both photographs and text stress safety and show correct equipment such as sun goggles and helmets. It is easy to see the differences in the course for a slalom, run between gates, and cross-country runs that go for miles along wooded trails. Special events, such as the biathlon, where competitors stop skiing to shoot at targets, are also explained in detail.

Among other equipment and snow sports discussed are: four-person bobsleds, a two-person luge, toboggans, skibobs, snowboards, skijoring, and dogsled racing. There is also a brief history of snow sports including the beginning of ski racing and the Winter Olympics.

Possible Topics for Further Student Investigation

1 Students may be surprised to learn that the history of skiing in America is closely tied to the California gold miners who began skiing to travel in the rugged, snowy mountain areas. The first official American ski club was formed in La Porte, California in 1867. With the help of a media specialist, ask a pair of interested students to research this topic. Which sources of information discuss skiing among the gold miners? Are there newspaper accounts? Are there any published photographs of skiers at this time? Have students give oral reports to the class about what they learn and explain how they carried out the research.

2 Skis, boots, bindings, poles, helmets, and goggles for skiers can be complex. Locate a local skier who would be willing to visit the class, bringing along ski equipment and explaining why the skis and poles are a certain length, why waxes are used, and why boots and bindings are designed the way they are.

3 The biathlon is unusual in that it combines target shooting and cross-country skiing. Ask a pair of interested students to research this topic. What is the history of this sport? When did it first become a major event? How far do these racers usually go, and how often do they stop to shoot? How far away are the targets? How are the racers scored? In past years, who have been the great champions in this sport? What records do they hold?

 *Weather & Climate*

by Mark Galan

Alexandria, VA: Time Life Books, 1992. 152p.

This book is part of a series called Understanding Science & Nature. It is large-format, illustrated mostly with color diagrams, but also contains a few color photographs. It is appropriate for students in grades four and five.

This is a rather comprehensive children's book on weather and climate with sections on: "The Air Above," "The Air in Motion," "Storm Machines," "Atmospheric Pressure," "Aerial Wonders," "Watching the Weather," and "The Climate System of Earth." It could prove useful throughout any unit on weather.

Of most interest to students involved in "snowy days" will be chapter 3, which discusses storm machines and specifically explains the causes of hail and snow, and chapter 6, which discusses weather forecasting.

Pages 74 and 75 graphically show what causes snow and hail. There are ice crystals in the upper layers of high cumulonimbus and altostratus clouds where temperatures are below freezing. These ice crystals rise and fall on air currents and bump into supercooled water droplets. The droplets attach to the ice crystals, forming larger crystals, and fall. If the ground temperature is below freezing, the crystals fall as snow. When the air currents inside the cloud are very strong, the ice crystals rise and fall several times within the cloud, continuing to grow, and finally become heavy enough to fall as hail.

Possible Projects for Further Student Investigation

1 Using simple materials, the teacher may want to conduct an experiment in class to show students how clouds form. Needed supplies include: two cups of very hot water, a two-cup Pyrex measuring cup, a five-inch square from an old nylon stocking, a rubber band, and six ice cubes. Pour hot water into a Pyrex measuring cup. When the cup becomes hot to the touch, pour out all but one inch of the water. Stretch the nylon fabric over the cup and fasten it with a rubber band. Put the ice cubes on top of the stocking. Water vapor will rise above the cup forming tiny clouds and drops of water will form on the inside of the cup. Students will see that clouds form when warm air rises and cools.

2 Pages 122 and 123 of this book explain that several nations maintain a total of 48 observation stations in Antarctica that transmit daily weather observations worldwide. Ask a group of interested students to further research this topic. Does the United States maintain one of these weather observatories? When was the first of these weather stations built? How many people live there? How long do they stay? How do they get there and get back out? Have students share what they learn with the class.

3 The National Weather Service provides forecasts and warnings of severe weather and floods for the United States. Ask a pair of interested students to find out more about the National Weather Service. When was it created? Where are its offices? Have them share what they learn with the class.

Winter Weather

by John Mason

New York: Bookwright Press, 1991. 32p.

This book is part of a series of books called Seasonal Weather. The series describes and explains the types of weather associated with each season of the year and how the weather affects people's activities in different parts of the world. It will appeal to children in grades three through five.

This book is illustrated with color photographs, charts, and drawings. It contains an index and a short glossary.

The book begins by explaining that winter is different in different parts of the world. In the tropics, people never see ice and snow. At the poles, it is bitterly cold all year. In the temperate regions of the earth, there are seasons. The temperate lands of the northern hemisphere have cold weather in December, January, and February, while people in the southern hemisphere are having summer weather at this time. The text explains, using drawings as well as text, why seasons occur.

In discussing winter weather, the author examines snow, hailstones, frost, fog, and monsoon winds. There are sections on: "Clouds and Water Vapor," "Snow, Fog and Frosts," "Cold Polar Lands," "Winter Around the World," "Very Cold Winters," "The Importance of the Oceans," "Ice Ages and Climatic Change," "Forecasting Winter Weather," and "Things to Do— Measuring Temperature."

The weather symbols shown on page 27 will help students record their own data as well as interpret weather data from weather maps that they see on television and in newspapers.

Possible Topics for Further Student Investigation

1 A small group of interested students might establish a classroom weather station. For one month of the year, these students might use symbols to record the type of weather that occurred each day, the high and low temperatures, wind speed and direction, and the barometric pressure in mid-morning and mid-afternoon. They might also make observations about the number and type of clouds visible in the sky. After a few weeks of recording data, students might try predicting the weather 24 hours in advance and compare their predictions to the actual weather.

2 One of our youngest states, Alaska, has a number of glaciers. With the help of your media specialist, ask a small group of students research Alaskan glaciers. Where are they located? Are some of these glaciers advancing or are they retreating? How fast are the glaciers moving? Try to locate some pictures of these glaciers. Have students report what they learn to the class.

3 Icebergs can be very dangerous to ships at sea. Ask a pair of students to read accounts of some shipwrecks caused by icebergs. They will learn about distress signals and Morse code. Have the students find a Morse code alphabet of dots and dashes and bring it to class. If possible, they should locate an amateur radio operator in your area who is licensed to broadcast code. Have the "ham radio operator" visit your class and demonstrate, using a "key," how code is sent.

Part IV

Sunny Days

Sunny Days

● FICTION ●

- *All I See*
- *Bawshou Rescues the Sun*
- *Born of the Sun*
- *Claude and Sun*
- *One Sun, A Book of Terse Verse*
- *Raven, A Trickster Tale from the Pacific Northwest*
- *The Sun, the Wind, and the Rain*
- *The Sun's Day*
- *Under the Sun*
- *When the Sun Rose*
- *Wild Wild Sunflower Child Anna*
- *The Wild Woods*

◆ BRIDGES ◆

- *Beach Days*
- *Summertime*

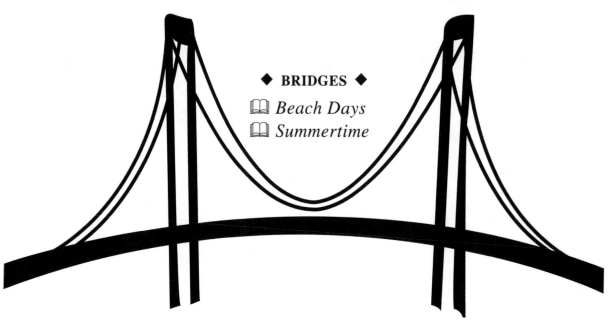

■ NONFICTION CONNECTIONS ■

- *The Amateur Meteorologist: Explorations and Investigations*
- *Autumn Weather*
- *Drought: The Past, Present, and Future Enemy*
- *Energy from Sun, Wind, and Tide*
- *Heat*
- *How Did We Find Out About Sunshine?*
- *I Can Be a Weather Forecaster*
- *Let's Celebrate Summer World Festivals*
- *Radiation*
- *Solar Power*
- *The Sun*
- *The Sun, Our Neatrest Star*

—OTHER TOPICS TO EXPLORE—

—Beaches	—Diving	—Heat	—Radiation
—Radio waves	—Solar power	—Solar system	—Summer festivals
—Sun gods	—Sun spots	—Surfboarding	—Swimming

From *Rainy, Windy, Snowy, Sunny Days*. © 1996. Teacher Ideas Press. (800) 237-6124.

Sunny Days

● *Fiction* ●

- 📖 *All I See*
- 📖 *Bawshou Rescues the Sun*
- 📖 *Born of the Sun*
- 📖 *Claude and Sun*
- 📖 *One Sun, A Book of Terse Verse*
- 📖 *Raven, A Trickster Tale from the Pacific Northwest*
- 📖 *The Sun, the Wind, and the Rain*
- 📖 *The Sun's Day*
- 📖 *Under the Sun*
- 📖 *When the Sun Rose*
- 📖 *Wild Wild Sunflower Child Anna*
- 📖 *The Wild Woods*

 *All I See*

FICTION

by Cynthia Ryland
Illustrated by Peter Catalanotto
New York: Orchard Books, 1988. 32p. (unnumbered)

This is a large-format picture book with full-color illustrations. It will be enjoyed by primary-grade students.

As the story opens, Gregory is painting beside a lake, whistling while he works. His white cat sits sleeping in the sun. When Gregory gets tired painting, he picks up his cat and the two of them drift on the water in a canoe.

A boy named Charlie visits this lake each summer. He watches Gregory paint. One day when Gregory is out in the canoe, Charlie comes by and looks at one of Gregory's paintings. He is surprised to see that it is a picture of a blue whale.

Charlie comes back often and always finds a whale, until one day he finds a blank canvas. So while Gregory is off in his canoe, Charlie picks up the paint brush and leaves a painting for Gregory. When Gregory returns, he is surprised to find a painting of himself and his cat.

The next day, when he and his cat, Stella, go out in the canoe, Gregory leaves a note for Charlie. And the next day, Gregory leaves another note, asking Charlie to stay. Charlie waits and the two meet. Gregory teaches Charlie about shadows, light, and line. One day Gregory gives Charlie his own easel, paints, brushes, and canvases. Then the two artists stand side by side and paint. When Charlie asks why Gregory only paints whales, he answers, "It's all I see."

Discussion Starters and Multidisciplinary Activities

1. Although they have never met, and Charlie has not even seen Gregory's painting when this story begins, Charlie is already fond of Gregory. Ask students why Charlie like a person he has not met?

2. Ask students if they were surprised that Charlie painted a picture and left it for Gregory. Would they have done that?

3. Ask students what they thought the picture would be when they saw Gregory painting a picture. Did they expect a whale, a scene at the lake, or a picture of Gregory? Why?

4. Gregory paints whales because he says that it is "all I can see." Allow students to use any media to draw their own favorite subject—whatever it is that they often see in their mind's eye. You might want to share these drawings on a class bulletin board with the caption "All I Can See."

5. Gregory chose to always paint a blue whale. Have a pair of students research blue whales. Where are they found? How big are they? What do they eat? How long does it take them to bear young? Do they migrate during the year? What are their major enemies? If possible, they might bring in a picture of a blue whale.

6. When summer ends, Gregory and Charlie return to their homes. Have students write a conversation in which one of these characters talks to someone else and tells that person about making a new friend. What would they say?

Bawshou Rescues the Sun

FICTION

by Chun-Chan Yeh and Allan Baillie
Illustrated by Michelle Powell
New York: Scholastic, 1991. 32p. (unnumbered)

This retelling of an old Chinese folk-tale is a large-format picture book with full-color illustrations. It will be enjoyed by students in the primary grades.

Liu Chun and his wife, Hui Niang, work a rice paddy near West Lake in eastern China. They are happily waiting for the birth of their first child. But one day, a wild wind comes and snatches the sun. When Liu Chun asks what has happened, an old man of the village explains that the King of the Devils, who is afraid of light, has stolen the sun and hidden it deep in his home.

Liu Chun, accompanied by a golden bird, sets off in search of the sun wearing a pair of shoes made by his wife. Hui Niang waits months for her husband. Her son, Bawshou, is born. One day, the bird returns alone, and a new star appears in the sky.

A breeze touches Bawshou, and he is full grown. The golden phoenix settles on his shoulder, and the two set off, following the star, to find the sun. Kindly villagers give Bawshou a warm cloak that keeps him afloat when he crosses the river. Other villagers feed him and give him a special parcel of earth. Bawshou avoids traps of the King of Devils and travels to the ocean where he uses pinches of earth to make islands so that he can cross the water. Bawshou creeps into a stone fortress and finds the dying sun in a cave deep under the sea. Freed, the sun grows in power and burns the King of Devils from the sky.

Discussion Starters and Multidisciplinary Activities

1. Before Liu Chun left to find the sun, a golden bird landed on his shoulder. He thought this was a good omen. Ask students if, at this point in the story, they thought Liu Chun would be successful or unsuccessful in rescuing the sun. Why?

2. Ask students why they think a lowly rice farmer, instead of a rich or powerful person, took on the task of rescuing the sun.

3. Villagers gave Bawshou the cloak that kept him from drowning in the river and the earth that let Bawshou create islands to cross the ocean. The phoenix warned Bawshou of danger and helped him along the way. Which do students think was most important to Bawshou's success, the villagers or the phoenix?

4. The phoenix has been used in many legends and stories. Ask a pair of students, with the help of the media specialist, to find another legend about the phoenix and share this new story with their classmates.

5. People in ancient times, who knew less about the sun, moon, and stars, became very frightened during eclipses of the sun. During such times, it seems that the sun has been "stolen from the sky." Ask a pair of students to study an eclipse of the sun or the moon and, using a flannel board, present an explanation to the class.

6. Someone in the community may have interesting things from China (slippers, clothing, paintings, etc.) that they might be willing to share with the class.

From *Rainy, Windy, Snowy, Sunny Days.* © 1996. Teacher Ideas Press. (800) 237-6124.

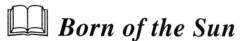 *Born of the Sun*

FICTION

by Gillian Cross
New York: Holiday House, 1983. 229p.

This is a chapter book that will be enjoyed by fourth- and fifth-grade readers. It is an adventure story written by an English author. Most of the story is set in Peru.

Karel is an explorer. He and his wife, Jean, take their daughter, Paula, out of school to join them in trying to find the lost city of Atahualpa, the son of the Sun, the last Inca to rule Peru. They take along with them a young photographer, Finn, and two native guides, Octavio and his son, Agustin.

From the beginning, Karel is impatient and in a rush. His actions are partly responsible for the first two mishaps of the journey, losing one of their mules, and causing their guide, Octavio, to fall to his death. Finn suggests that they give up the expedition and return home. But when a vote is taken, Karel, Jean, and Paula vote to continue.

The climbing, dangerous water falls, hacking a path, and worry about the accuracy of the directions they are following are hard on the travelers. But most difficult is Karel's strange behavior. His daughter is reluctant to believe that Karel is sick or out of his mind.

Jean finally tells the others that Karel has cancer but that she could not deny him this one last trip. He is unconscious when they carry him into a village of the Kallawaya's where a medicine man says perhaps he can work a cure, but only if the travelers have faith and believe in him.

Discussion Starters and Multidisciplinary Activities

1. The story opens and closes with Paula talking with one of her school friends, Fettis. Ask students why they think the author chose to include these two scenes?

2. Everyone who made this strange journey to the Kallawaya's village changed in some way on the trip. Have students describe the changes they noticed in the various characters.

3. Paula and Jean come to know and see each other differently during this journey. Have students discuss how they think this newfound understanding will be shown once mother and daughter are back in England?

4. Have students locate Lake Titicaca on a map of Peru. This is close to where Karel's expedition was headed. They should also locate London and Bolivia, the cities to and from which the explorers flew.

5. Have a small group of interested students research Pizarro's expeditions to Peru. When did they take place? How many Spanish explorers were involved? Where did they travel, and what did they find? Have these students share what they learn with the class.

6. Although villages, trails, and bridges in this area had all but vanished, the one thing that helped Karel believe he could follow the old directions was the existence of rivers. Ask a pair of students to research rivers in Peru and make a map of the country naming and showing the major rivers. When complete, hang the map on a class bulletin board.

 *Claude and Sun*

FICTION

by Matt Novak
New York: Bradbury Press, 1987. 32p. (unnumbered)

This picture book has minimal text and is illustrated with Impressionist-inspired, full-color drawings. This story will be enjoyed by kindergarten and first-grade students. Older students might be intrigued with the special techniques used in the illustrations.

As the story opens, Claude is walking and soaking in the sunshine. He takes off his jacket and begins to work in his garden. Vegetables are thriving here, and Claude does not seem the least unhappy that there are rabbits enjoying his garden too.

Also in the garden is a patch of giant sunflowers. The sun and Claude play peek-a-boo with the flowers and both dance across the pond where there are frogs and water lilies.

Leaving his garden, Claude, accompanied by the sun, goes into the forest, where he picks berries and finds a secret passage way to a "rain spot" where everyone is huddled beneath umbrellas. Claude and the sun are made welcome. They play hide-and-go-seek among the clouds and umbrellas until it is almost dark. Then Claude waves good-bye and leaves. He walks home through the sunlight at the end of the day.

Claude gets ready for bed and snuggles beneath the covers just as the sun is getting ready to set. The two say good-night as darkness falls.

Discussion Starters and Multidisciplinary Activities

1 Ask the students to describe what they notice about Claude, in the first few pictures, that lets them know what kind of a person he is. Have them look at the expression on Claude's face and at his actions.

2 Instead of showing it simply start to rain, the author/artist shows Claude discovering a secret passage that leads to a "rain spot." Have students discuss why the author might have done this.

3 The sun and Claude played peek-a-boo and hide-and-go-seek. Ask students if they can think of another game that Claude and the sun might have played. Have students tell about these new games and what sorts of pictures might have illustrated these games.

4 Ask your art educator to visit the class and show students reproductions from some of the famous Impressionist painters. Compare their work to the type of illustrations used in this story. What techniques are used?

5 With the help of the art educator, have students create a work of art in an Impressionist style. Share this artwork on a classroom bulletin board.

6 Claude is very different in his approach from the famous Farmer McGregor in the story of Peter Rabbit. Reread Peter's adventures to the students. Then have student volunteers act out a conversation in which Claude tries to persuade Farmer McGregor to be more sympathetic toward rabbits.

 *One Sun, A Book of Terse Verse*

FICTION

by Bruce McMillan
New York: Holiday House, 1990. 32p. (unnumbered)

This book, illustrated with photographs taken at the beach in Maine, is a book of terse verse. Each page contains either two rhyming words or a picture illustrating the pair of words. It will be enjoyed by primary-grade students.

Terse verse is composed of two monosyllabic words that need not be spelled similarly, but must sound alike, such as the title of this book, *One Sun*. This book uses terse verse to show a day with children at the beach.

The title page for *One Sun* sets the scene by showing a young boy playing in the water. This is followed by "Sand Hand," where a photograph illustrates the verse by showing only the boy's hand, which is covered with grains of sand.

The boy and other playmates are then shown hopping on a "lone stone," tracing through the sand a "snail trail," building a sort of breakwater with "six sticks," playing with a "small ball," playing fetch with a dog who is a "wet pet," seeing the lifeguard who is a "tan man," sitting with the guard in his tower on a "neat seat," playing with a dump truck in the sand until it is a "stuck truck," pouring water into a "whale pail," using trowels in the sand in a "scoop group," patting the sand into a large "round mound," enjoying a cool "pink drink," and finally flying a "white kite."

Just a few words capture the fun of a day at the beach.

Discussion Starters and Multidisciplinary Activities

1 Only a few words are used, but rhyme and photographs capture vivid images of the activities. After reading the story, close the book, and challenge students to recall as many of the terse verses as they can. List these on the board.

2 In "scoop group" and "round mound," the boy in the story seems to be talking to the girl. Ask students to suggest what the boy might be saying.

3 Have students suggest names that might be appropriate for the "wet pet" shown in this book. Why they would give the dog these names?

4 Students might want to invent riddles and try them on their classmates. Explain that all answers for these riddles must be in rhyme. For example, a child might say, "I'm thinking of a ridiculous rabbit. What is it, using two syllable words?" The answer would be a "funny bunny." Or a student might say, "I'm thinking of something hard to climb. What is it, using one syllable words?" The answer would be "tall wall."

5 Choose a theme for a book and have each class member contribute a page of terse verse and illustration. Instead of a day at the beach, this might be a trip through the zoo, a picnic, or a day in the woods.

6 Once your class book (or books) are complete, choose pairs of students to visit other primary-grade classes and read the book.

FICTION

📖 *Raven, A Trickster Tale from the Pacific Northwest*

by Gerald McDermott

San Diego, CA: Harcourt Brace Jovanovich, 1993. 32p. (unnumbered)

This picture book is brightly illustrated in full color and is a retelling of a traditional Native American legend. It will be enjoyed by primary-grade readers.

As the story begins, the world and all the people are in darkness. Raven feels sorry for them and decides to search for light. Raven flies over mountains, rivers, and lakes. He finally sees a bit of light at the edge of some water.

The light is coming from the house of Sky Chief. Raven perches in a pine tree to watch. He sees Sky Chief's daughter come out. She drinks some water from a woven basket. Raven quickly changes himself into a pine needle and falls into the water just in time for the girl to drink and swallow him.

Later, the young girl has a child. It is Raven who has been reborn as Raven-child. Sky Chief loves his grandson and plays with him. All the time that Raven-child crawls and plays, he is trying to find out where the light is hidden.

Raven-child sees a glowing box. The young girl gives it to Raven-child. She takes off the lid. There is another box inside; and another and another. Inside the smallest box is a shining ball, the sun. Sky Chief tells his daughter to give the ball to Raven-child. As soon as he has the ball, Raven-child becomes a bird and flies away with the sun. Raven throws the sun into the sky where it stays, giving light to all the people.

Discussion Starters and Multidisciplinary Activities

1. Ask students to tell you why it is so easy for readers to understand that the young woman's baby is really Raven.

2. Ask students if they noticed what happened to the sounds that Raven-child made and how they changed. (He began saying "Ga-Ga," then said "Ha! Ha!," and finally, "Caw! Caw!")

3. Because everyone in Sky Chief's house was very kind to Raven-child, should he have stolen the sun? Why or why not?

4. The front matter of the book tells that Raven is a common figure in Native American folklore and is often a "trickster." With the help of a media specialist, ask a pair of students to find another legend involving Raven and read it to the class.

5. Totem poles of the Northwest often feature Raven. Ask a pair of students to find books or magazines with pictures of totem poles. Have them bring these pictures to the class and explain which part of the totem depicts Raven.

6. Students could make totem poles, including not only Raven, but Beaver, Eagle, Frog, and other symbols. One large totem could be made for the classroom, or students could each make a small one. Many objects can be used for basic large totems: tubes from inside rolls of carpets, a stack of empty cardboard ice cream tubs. For small totems, use tubes from rolls of wrapping paper. The designs can be done with poster paints, magic markers, construction paper, and so on. A "wing" across the totem could be cut from cardboard and stapled in place.

From *Rainy, Windy, Snowy, Sunny Days.* © 1996. Teacher Ideas Press. (800) 237-6124.

The Sun, the Wind, and the Rain

 FICTION

by Lisa Westberg Peters
Illustrated by Ted Rand
New York: Henry Holt, 1988. 32p. (unnumbered)

This picture book will appeal to primary-grade readers. It is brightly illustrated with full-color pictures. It not only tells a simple story, but it also serves as an introduction to geology.

This book tells of two mountains. The earth made its mountain millions of years ago, beginning with a fiery, hot underground pool that grew cold and then rockhard. Elizabeth makes her small mountain today, at the beach, in a few minutes using a bucket of wet sand. Earth's mountain grew slowly as the earth shifted, and the mountain rose. Elizabeth's mountain grows quickly as she piles on more sand and pats it smooth.

Trees, flowers, and animals live on the earth's mountain. Elizabeth puts sticks and pebbles on hers. Earth's mountain is exposed to hundreds of years of weather. Elizabeth's sand mountain bakes in the afternoon sun. Breezes blow some of the sand away. Rainstorms crumbled part of earth's mountain. An afternoon shower washes away much of Elizabeth's mountain.

Earth's mountain's jagged peaks disappeared and it became rounded. Elizabeth's mountain becomes a bump on the beach. Over time, the layers washed from the mountain may rise to form another mountain. Elizabeth uses the sand that washed from her mountain to rebuild another one before she leaves the beach.

Discussion Starters and Multidisciplinary Activities

1   Explain to students that this is a parallel story, that two stories are taking place at once. Have them tell you what the two story lines are.

2   Ask students if they have been at a beach and had a chance to make a mountain or sand castle. Allow time to share these experiences.

3   Elizabeth is all alone in this story. Have students discuss whether the story might have been more or less interesting if she had friends or family with her.

4   Students may not know much about geology. Ask a local geologist to visit the class and talk with students about the work of geologists. If possible, the guest should bring specimens to share. Help the students to prepare questions ahead of time for the guest speaker.

5   To demonstrate erosion, put several samples of different kinds of rough rocks in a coffee can with a plastic cover. Give each student the opportunity to vigorously shake the can for a minute or two. Then examine the contents. Dust and sand will be in the can from breaking off of the larger rocks.

6   Invite students to gather and bring in samples of sand collected from different spots (the playground, back yard, a near by stream, the beach). Make slides to study under a microscope. Punch a hole in an index card and cover it with tape. Stick some sand on the tape. Cover the other side with tape. Can you see differences?

 *The Sun's Day*

FICTION

by Mordicai Gerstein
New York: Harper & Row, 1989. 32p. (unnumbered)

This picture book has full-color illustrations and minimal text. It will appeal to primary-grade readers.

This book describes hours of the day, and in each picture the sun has a special role. At five o'clock in the morning, the sun creeps above the mountains. At six, the sun is pictured as a yellow chick hatching out of an egg, and at seven o'clock, the sun is a fretful baby waking up and crying for breakfast.

At eight o'clock, the sun resembles a pat of butter dripping on a piece of breakfast toast. At nine, the sun is a collection of horns and bells that announce the day's activities. At ten o'clock, the sun is a giant sunflower with bees buzzing around it. At eleven o'clock, with cars, trucks, and factories in full swing, the sun is a set of wheels and gears.

At noon, when people stop for lunch, the sun is a big, round sandwich. By one o'clock, the sun is a cat that is curled up and napping. At two o'clock, the sun looks like a giant peach, ripe and ready to pick. Three o'clock shows children on the playground while the sun is a collection of balls, and at four, the sun is a design on a kite flying in the sky.

At five o'clock, the sun is a simmering pot of soup, and by six, the sun is a collection of paints that could be used in a sunset. By seven, the sun sets on the water like a baby taking its bath, and at eight, the sun goes down, and night begins.

Discussion Starters and Multidisciplinary Activities

1. Have students to pick our their favorite illustration and explain why it is their favorite.

2. Point out that not only is the sun taking on special forms, but that the clouds resemble objects, too. Ask them to look at an illustration and tell what the clouds resemble.

3. This story tells something that might happen at each hour during a day. With the students, brainstorm other activities that often take place at a certain time of day that are not shown in this book.

4. Students may want to add an illustration to the book. Ask them to draw a typical scene in which the sun has taken on a special form.

5. One scene in the book depicts a fruit stand, not far from a peach orchard, by a road near the water. Have a pair of students research where most peaches are grown in the United States. Have them share what they learn with the class.

6. People who live in other lands might have a very different daily routine from the one shown in this book. As a group activity, brainstorm the outline for a book reflecting what might be happening in another country at the various hours of the day. A pair of interested students might volunteer to write and illustrate such a book to share with the class.

 # Under the Sun

FICTION

by Ellen Kandoian
New York: Dodd, Mead, 1987. 28p. (unnumbered)

This picture book, with its soft, full-color illustrations, will appeal to kindergarten and first-grade students. It has minimal text.

When the story begins, Molly, who lives on the East Coast, asks her mother where the sun goes at night. Mother answers that the sun goes to the Mississippi River, where a little boy watches it set from his houseboat. From there, it goes to the Great Plains where a girl sees it set over the prairie. It continues to the Rocky Mountains, and then to San Francisco.

Next the sun goes to Hawaii, where children watch it go down over the Pacific Ocean. It goes to Japan, where a girl watches it set from her garden, and then on China, where a panda watches it disappear among the trees.

Next it goes to the Mongolian Desert, where a camel sees it set behind the dunes, and to Russia, where a little boy might be wondering, just as Molly wonders, what happens to the sun when he goes to bed. Mother explains that in the morning, while it is on its rounds, the sun will come in Molly's window and wake her.

The book concludes with a one-page explanation of sunlight and darkness and suggests using a globe and a flashlight in a darkened room to show that as the globe turns, one spot moves from light into darkness.

Discussion Starters and Multidisciplinary Activities

1 Ask students if they can remember asking questions about day and night. How did someone explain the rotation of the earth and the causes night and day.

2 Instead of telling about the rotation of the earth, Molly's mother explains day and night by choosing places around the globe as the sun sets. Using a globe, have students locate the places mentioned.

3 After reading the story, ask students if they can remember the one where the sun was not shining because it was raining (San Francisco). Ask students why they think the author included a rainy spot in the story.

4 Students may want to carry out the activity explained on the final page of the book. While sitting in a circle in a darkened room around a large globe, one student can slowly turn the globe while another student holds a flashlight shining on the globe. Students will see how an area moves in and out of sunlight.

5 A pair of interested students might want to write and illustrate a similar picture book entitled *Under the Moon*. They might share their finished story with the class.

6 If students were interested in the explanation of day and night, this might be a good time to discuss why we have seasons. Ask a pair of students to research this and then explain their findings to the class. They might draw pictures or use a flannel board in their presentation.

 *When the Sun Rose*

FICTION

by Barbara Helen Berger
New York: Philomel Books, 1986. 32p. (unnumbered)

This is a picture book, illustrated in bold primary colors, with a simple text that will appeal to primary-grade readers.

The story begins at sunrise when a friend comes to visit a young girl. The reader realizes that this friend is special because she comes in a bright carriage pulled by a golden lion.

The lion stops at the girl's door, and the visitor, a girl with golden hair wearing a gown of yellow flowers, is invited in. When the girl enters the house, her lion comes with her, and his feet are as silent as sunlight.

The girls and their dolls have a tea party, enjoying honeycake and tea while the lion has blueberries with cream.

The girls play. They change the clothes on their dolls, and they read books while the lion purrs.

They paint a picture of a rainbow and pass a happy day playing together. At sunset, it is time for the friend to say goodbye.

The girl asks if her friend will return. And the friend promises to do so. As shadows appear, the girl watches her friend going home in her golden carriage.

It is dark, and the girl goes back into her house. Although her friend is gone, the girl is sure her friend will keep her promise and come again, because the rainbow in the picture they made shines on the wall, and the house is full of roses.

Discussion Starters and Multidisciplinary Activities

1 Ask the students to think about the title of this book, *When the Sun Rose*, and the first picture in the book, depicting the sun as a big yellow rose. Discuss the two meanings of the word *rose*.

2 In the second picture shown in the book, a tree prevents the reader from seeing what is in the center of the rose and who is coming to visit. Ask students who or what they thought might be sitting in the carriage.

3 Each of the girls has a doll, and the dolls seem to hold hands. They also trade dresses. Have the students discuss the roles that the dolls play in this story.

4 Words can be spelled exactly the same way but have two different meanings, such as the word *rose*, which is used in the title of this book. Or, words can sound alike but be spelled differently and have different meanings such as *blew* and *blue*. Have students think of a word with two meanings and then draw two pictures showing the different meanings.

5 Have two students research the sun and report some interesting number facts to the class. How far away is the sun? What is its diameter? How long does it take light from the sun to reach earth?

6 Students interested in the topic might try to find out and tell the class what time it is in Paris, France; in London, England; in Tokyo, Japan; in Sydney, Australia; and in New Delhi, India when it is noon at your school.

Wild Wild Sunflower Child Anna

FICTION

by Nancy White Carlstrom
Illustrated by Jerry Pinkney
New York: Macmillan, 1987. 32p. (unnumbered)

This is a picture book with full-color illustrations that will appeal to primary-grade students. The story uses a lot of rhyming words and is poem-like in its construction.

In the morning, Anna, a little girl dressed in yellow and resembling a sunflower, is running and jumping. She spins around with her arms open wide until she is dizzy. Finally, she falls to the ground among the flowers.

While she is on the ground, Anna plays with a dandelion's seeds and sifts the soil lightly through her fingers. Next, it is berry picking time. Anna picks the ripe, juicy berries that come off easily from the vine and gets some berry juice on her nose. Then Anna takes off her shoes and runs barefoot. The burrs stick to her shoulders and get in her hair, but she does not care as she skips about.

Then Anna goes to the creek where she hops from rock to rock and looks at the great, green frogs that live there. A frog jumps and splashes Anna's legs. Anna goes to the top of a hill and climbs a tree, pretending she is a captain of a ship.

Anna rolls down the hill, coming back to the garden where the story began, standing next to the wild sunflowers. Anna notices the ants, the buzzing bees, and the spiders spinning webs. As the trees sway and the breeze blows, Anna closes her eyes and falls asleep in the grass.

Discussion Starters and Multidisciplinary Activities

1 There is a lot of rhyme used throughout this poetic story. Read a page to the students and have them point out which words rhyme.

2 Because Anna is dressed in a yellow dress, she resembles the sunflowers. Ask students if they can think of other ways in which Anna resembles the wild sunflowers.

3 Anna is all alone in this story. We know nothing about her family or where she lives. We do not know how far she is from home. Ask students to discuss why the author chose to have Anna completely on her own.

4 Sunflowers grow quickly and are sturdy plants. Their seeds are favorites with some birds and animals. If possible allow students to each grow a sunflower plant in a small milk carton filled with good soil. They can take the plants home when they have sprouted and plant them in their gardens.

5 Anna notices a spider making a web. Have a pair of interested students research spider webs. Are all webs alike? Do all spiders make webs? Is part of a web sticky? Why does the spider not stick to her web? Have them report what they learn to the class.

6 Favorite berries are raspberries, strawberries, blueberries, and blackberries. As a special treat, hold a berry party. If fresh berries are not available for tasting, bring in jars of jam so that students can taste them and try to describe the differences among the various available berries.

 *The Wild Woods*

FICTION

by Simon James

Cambridge, MA: Candlewick Press, 1993. 28p. (unnumbered)

This is a picture book filled with comical, watercolor illustrations that will appeal to primary-grade students.

This book describes a day in the forest. The story begins as Jess walks with Grandad and they meet a squirrel that Jess would like to take home with her. Grandad explains that they cannot keep the squirrel because it is too wild.

Jess goes after the squirrel anyway, saying that she will take care of him. The squirrel runs through the trees and across a stream. Jess is right behind the squirrel, and Grandad tries to keep up with them. When Grandad asks what she will feed the squirrel, Jess says that he likes sandwiches. She and the squirrel are seated having a picnic together.

While Grandad wrings out the socks that he got wet in the creek, he asks where the squirrel will sleep if they take him home. Jess says she will make him a bed in her room. She is already in pursuit of the squirrel again, this time climbing across a long log and then up the muddy creek bank.

Grandad loses a shoe in the mud and Jess urges him to hurry because she has found a waterfall. They sit by the falls and rest. Grandad again explains that they cannot keep the squirrel. This time Jess agrees. She says she knows that it belongs in the wild.

Jess says she likes being in the woods and asks if they can come back tomorrow, as the ducks might need taking care of.

Discussion Starters and Multidisciplinary Activities

1 There are many amusing illustrations in this book. Ask students to pick out some of their favorites and explain why they find these particularly funny.

2 Have students explain how they think Jess and Grandad feel about each other. What occurs in the story that leads the students to think as they do?

3 Ask students if they think Grandad will bring Jess back to the wild woods again soon, and if so, what they think might happen on their next visit?

4 Jess wishes she could have a squirrel for a pet. Most students wish that they could have a pet of some kind. Ask students to draw a picture of a pet that they have or one that they would like to have. Share these with the class.

5 Jess is willing to care for the squirrel, but she does not know a lot about squirrels. Have a pair of students do some research. Where do squirrels sleep at night? What do they usually eat? Are there different kinds of squirrels? What kind or kinds of squirrels live in your area? Have these students report what they learn to the class.

6 Squirrels are curious creatures and frequently get into mischief. They take strings from mops for their nests and sometimes chew through telephone lines. They make great leaps through the trees. Ask students to write a poem or short story that features a squirrel. Put these on a class bulletin board and allow time for sharing.

 ***Bridges***

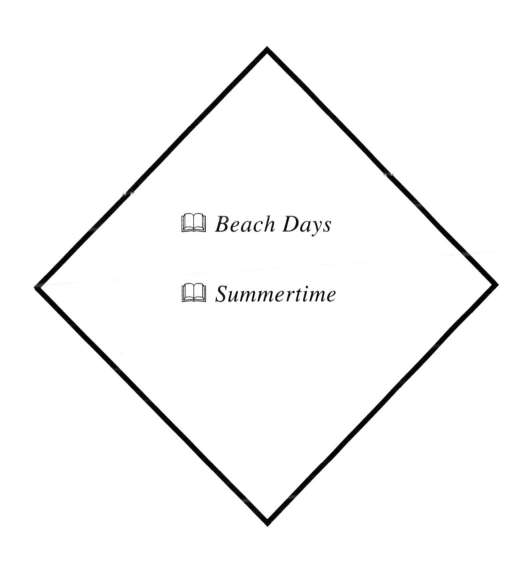

📖 *Beach Days*

📖 *Summertime*

📖 *Beach Days*

BRIDGES

by Ken Robbins
New York: Viking Kestrel, 1987. 28p. (unnumbered)

This bridge book is a realistic presentation of what a day at the beach might be like. Primary-grade students will enjoy the book, and older students might be interested in the technique used to produce these unusual pictures. The photos were shot in black and white and hand-colored using watercolor dyes.

The book begins by stating that not every day is a beach day. Sometimes it is cold or raining, or the waves are too high. But other days, when the air is warm and school is out, people head for the beach.

When people come to the beach, some come alone, and others come with friends and family. They often bring things with them: surfboards, rafts, inner tubes, beach balls, and kites. Some people try to find a spot where they can be alone on the beach while others prefer crowds.

Some people like to build castles or dig in the sand. Some enjoy hot dogs and ice cream. Some walk along the shallow water and others run along the water's edge. Some jump right into the surf and swim. Others go out into the water on their surfboard, while some try to catch the wind on their sailboard. Some people watch boats go by and others sail their own little boats. Others play games like beach volleyball or float in their inner tubes. Some just sit and watch.

Possible Topics for Further Student Investigation

1 The illustrations in this book are unusual They were shot in black-and-white and printed on lifospeed black-and-white paper. Then they were hand-colored by the author, using watercolor dyes. Most students will be familiar with black-and-white photos and with color photography, but probably not with tinting. Ask a local photographer to visit the class and explain the process of developing and printing film. If the guest is familiar with the technique, ask for an explanation of hand tinting.

2 A student may want to try an experiment to show roughly how a camera works. Cut a one-inch square in the bottom of a clean oatmeal box. Tape a piece of aluminum foil over the one-inch square. Prick a hole into the middle of the foil using a fine needle. Tape a piece of tissue paper over the open end of the oatmeal box. Point the pinhole out the window of a room into bright sunlight at a house or tree across the street. You will be able to see an image of the house or tree, upside down, on the piece of tissue paper.

3 Invite to class a beach enthusiast to discuss water sports. This person might bring along a surfboard, a sailboard, or flippers and goggles. Ask the guest to talk about what he or she does at the beach, to talk about any special equipment that is needed, the desirable wind and water conditions that may be necessary to this sport, and any special techniques that are used in the sport.

Summertime

by Anne Schweninger

New York: Viking Penguin, 1992. 32p. (unnumbered)

This bridge book gives a wealth of information about the events of summer. It is a part of the Let's Look at the Seasons Series and will be enjoyed by second- and third-grade readers.

This book begins with the first day of summer in June when the sun rises earlier and sets later than on any other day of the year. The text explains that summer is a time for growth. Pictured are a deer, ducks, turtles, and frogs who enjoy the plentiful food of summertime.

The short section on summer flowers discusses pollination and describes the hummingbirds, butterflies, and bees that sip nectar from blossom centers.

Information is given about the growth of trees, the life cycle of a monarch butterfly, and the fact that sometimes in summer there may be a heat wave. Readers are cautioned to wear protective sunscreen and sunglasses. There is also a section on thunderstorm safety, which gives tips on what one should do if caught outside during a thunderstorm.

Fun summer activities are also promoted, such as visiting the library for summer reading, making ice pops with fruit juice, going to the beach, camping in the backyard, getting to know the summer night sky, planting and tending a garden, and harvesting crops before summer ends.

Possible Topics for Further Student Investigation

1 Early in this book there is a picture of painted turtles sunning themselves on a log. There are many different kinds of turtles, some of which do better than others when kept in vivariums at home and at school. Ask a pair of students who are interested in turtles to make an appointment and then to go to a pet shop interview the owner to find out which turtles make the best pets, what sort of living quarters they need, what they eat, and other useful facts. Have these students report what they learn to the class.

2 Ask a pair of interested students to prepare a report on various kinds of hummingbirds to share with the class. The media specialist might help them identify various magazines that specialize in photographs of birds and locate issues with articles about hummingbirds. The students should include drawings or pictures of the different kinds of hummingbirds, as well as describe their size, eggs, nests, food, and so on.

3 Invite a guest speaker to talk about the care of skin in summertime. This person might be a dermatologist or other knowledgeable person. The speaker could explain the various numbers that designate different sunscreens and lotions and could discuss what sort of protection might be appropriate for different student summer activities such as hiking, swimming, boating, and so on. Students should prepare a list of questions ahead of time and should have the responsibility for writing a follow-up thank-you letter.

Sunny Days

Nonfiction Connections

The Amateur Meteorologist: Explorations and Investigations

NONFICTION CONNECTIONS

by H. Michael Mogil and Barbara G. Levine

New York: Franklin Watts, 1993. 128p.

The Amateur Meteorologist: Explorations and Investigations is one of the Amateur Science Series, which encourages students to observe, record, collect, classify, and experiment. Although it might be helpful in any of the four major sections of this book, it is included here. Chapter three, "Sun and Seasons," will be particularly relevant. It will be most useful to students in grades three through five.

This book encourages students to collect weather folklore and then test it to see if it contains some truth. For example, one old saying goes, "When clouds appear like rocks and towers, the earth's refreshed by frequent showers."

This book contains useful information on the water cycle, cloud formation, pressure, and wind. It gives students information about identifying different kinds of clouds, reading weather maps, calculating the dew point and relative humidity, and determining the windchill factor.

Of most interest to elementary students and teachers will be the detailed instructions on how to build simple and basic weather instruments such as a wind vane, thermometer, barometer, rain gauge, and anemometer.

There are also numerous suggestions for hands-on investigations. Most of these use simple and inexpensive materials and could lead students into more long-range science fair projects.

Possible Topics for Further Student Investigation

1. Teachers in grades three through five are often seeking ways to give students reasons to practice their graphing skills. Many aspects of weather lend themselves to graphing projects and allow students a visual means of presenting the data that they collect. Page 22 of this text shows three graphs that correlate temperature, pressure, and precipitation over a one-week period. After explaining how each of these three graphs was constructed, encourage two students to graph and show a similar correlation of these weather factors for a period of time and to share their graphs with the class.

2. A simple heat experiment could be carried out by class members at school during a sunny day. Fill four heavy-duty plastic zip-lock bags half full of water. Place these bags in four different spots: one in the sun on the blacktop, one in the sun on grass, one in the sun on a piece of white paper on the ground, and one in a shady location. Ask students to predict which bags of water will be coolest and hottest. Wait one hour and then measure the temperature of the water in the three bags. Were class predictions correct?

3. Sometimes meteorologists from local or nearby television or radio stations are willing to visit classrooms and speak with students. Investigate this possibility. Have a pair of students contact a meteorologist and try to arrange for a visit. Prepare questions ahead of time. Give students the responsibility for thanking the guest verbally and in writing.

From *Rainy, Windy, Snowy, Sunny Days.* © 1996. Teacher Ideas Press. (800) 237-6124.

Autumn Weather

by John Mason

New York: Bookwright Press, 1991. 32p.

Autumn Weather is part of the Seasonal Weather Series, which describes the types of weather associated with each season of the year and explains how weather affects human activities. This book is approximately half text and half color photographs and drawings. It will be enjoyed by students in grades two to four.

This book begins with a discussion of the seasons and why they occur. This is followed by details about the autumn season. Autumn is presented as a season of changes.

Information is provided about the earth's winds, fog, frost, and the formation of clouds. There is detailed information about weather satellites, weather maps and forecasts.

The section on drought and famine shows the effect of severe weather on crops.

When high pressure regions stray too far north or too far south from their usual pattern and remain too long in one position, and this is repeated for several years in a row, a drought may occur. When the rainfall is consistently lower than normal, crops may fail and famines result.

For students studying "sunny days," the section of *Autumn Weather* that is called "Blue Skies and Red Sunsets" will be of particular interest. The text explains that sunlight is white light made up of the seven colors of the spectrum. Each of the colors has a different wavelength. The blue skies that we associate with sunny, summer days are the result of blue light being scattered more than any other.

Possible Topics for Further Student Investigation

1 In the temperate regions, there are annual times in the fall when tree leaves change colors. Depending on where you live, there may be golds or bright reds. This change in leaf color would make an interesting topic for a pair of students to research. Why do leaves turn red, yellow, and brown? Why does this happen at a particular time of year? Have students research the topic and share with the class what they learn.

2 A simple but interesting art project can be done using an iron, an ironing board, a paper punch, waxed paper, some yarn, and a collection of leaves. Have each student collect small, brightly colored leaves and bring them to class. Give each student a sheet of waxed paper approximately 6 inches square. Have the students fold the paper in half and then arrange leaves inside the fold, like a "sandwich." Using a low setting, and being careful to avoid burns, iron the waxed paper with the leaves between the sheets. Using a paper punch, make a hole near one end. Thread through the hole and knot a bright piece of yarn. Trim your bookmark to size.

3 Many poems have been written about autumn leaves, including Robert Frost's "Gathering Leaves." Read some poems about autumn to the class. Ask students to reflect on the beauty of autumn leaves and then write their own nature poems. Share these on a class bulletin board or gather them into a class book of autumn poetry.

📖 *Drought: The Past, Present, and Future Enemy*

by Edward F. Dolan
New York: Franklin Watts, 1990. 144p.

NONFICTION CONNECTIONS

This book has 10 chapters and is illustrated with a few black-and-white photographs. It is appropriate for students in grades four and five.

The book begins with a look at various times and places throughout the world when there have been droughts. It is explained that droughts are enemies that do not strike suddenly with fury like a tornado or hurricane. Rather, droughts seem to sneak up on people. Their causes are complex.

Drought can cause death. With the loss of water, crops and livestock die, and famine strikes. It is estimated that, as a result of the drought that struck the Sahel in northern Africa in the 1960s and 1970s, 100,000 people died.

Chapter three explains why drought strikes. Winds can bring on droughts by altering force or shifting direction. Atmospheric pressure affects drought when factors create permanent high pressure areas. And there are permanent high pressure areas over the oceans that affect climate.

Other chapters discuss the unending drought cycles, the dirty thirties, ways to fight drought, including weather modification, and actions to conquer this enemy in the future.

To combat drought, the author argues that everyone must be involved in protecting our atmosphere, ending deforestation, and working for better methods of preserving our water supplies.

The book concludes with an extensive bibliography.

Possible Topics for Further Student Investigation

1. This book discusses the droughts that have struck at different times and places throughout the world. Have a pair of students mount a large world map on the bulletin board. Place numbered flags on the map to indicate spots where there has been severe drought. Then, prepare a chart placed beneath the map on which they list the numbered flags and identify the time and place of each drought along with any pertinent information such as loss of lives, crops, cattle, and so on.

2. This book mentions some interesting international activities and groups, including the World Meteorological Organization and the International Council of Scientific Unions, which are working on such problems as pollution and the greenhouse effect. With the help of a media specialist, ask two students to find the current addresses of these two organizations. Then have the students write, sending a stamped, self-addressed 9-by-12-inch envelope, and ask for materials that may be available from these two groups. Share the materials with the class.

3. In the 1970s, the U.S. Congress enacted the Clean Air Act. Ask members of the class to write to your senators requesting a copy of the Act and any information or reports that may be available describing what your state has been doing with respect to complying with that Act. When the materials arrive, spend some time discussing them. Is there a problem in your state with respect to clean air? Are some cities or some industries in your state in violation of the Act?

📖 *Energy from Sun, Wind, and Tide*

by Jacqueline Dineen
Hillside, NJ: Enslow, 1988. 32p.

This book is illustrated with color photographs. It is part of a series of books, The World's Harvest, which examines global resources. It will be of interest to students in grades two through four.

This book has four chapters: "What Is Energy?," "Power from the Sun," "Power from the Wind," and "Power from the Sea." Although all sections will be of interest to those who are concerned about alternative energy sources, the chapter "Power from the Sun" will be focused on here.

The section on solar power describes three ways in which power from the sun works. The simplest method is making direct use of the heat that the sun provides, which is called passive solar heating. This involves nothing more than trapping and storing the sun's energy. Active solar heating requires equipment designed to trap and circulate the heat efficiently. The third means involves converting sunshine into electricity by using solar cells called photovoltaic cells.

An example of passive solar heating is a house designed with large south-facing windows with dark colors inside to absorb more heat. In active solar heating systems, solar collectors trap and store the heat, which is then distributed by pumps and fans. Solar cells, or photovoltaic cells, which were developed in the 1940s, are made of silicon and they turn the energy from the sun into electricity.

Possible Topics for Further Student Investigation

1. Page 16 of *Energy from Sun, Wind, and Tide* shows solar cells. This is an interesting process of using the sun's energy, and students may need further explanation than that provided in this brief section. If someone in your community who works with solar power is willing to speak to a class of young students, invite that person to explain further how photovoltaic cells work and how these cells might be used now and in the future.

2. In Chapter two, "What Is Energy?" there is a very brief discussion of an English scientist, Michael Faraday, who discovered that moving a wire through a magnetic field produces an electric current. Ask a pair of students who show interest in this area to research the topic. Have them find out more about Michael Faraday and his work. See if the students can devise a simple, safe experiment in which they can show the class how a small amount of electricity can be produced using wire and a magnet.

3. Sunlight warms the earth. Students can make a solar still to show this. Dig a hole in damp soil about 18 inches wide and 1 foot deep. Place a bowl in the bottom of the hole. Cover the hole with clear plastic. Drop a small rock onto the plastic so that it sags down, about two inches above the bowl. Fasten the plastic in place all around the hole with using dirt and rocks. The sun will cause moisture to evaporate from the soil, condense into water droplets on the plastic, and then drip into the bowl.

Heat

by Neil Ardley
New York: Heinemann, 1991. 48p.

This book is part of a series called The Way It Works, and will be enjoyed by third- through fifth-grade readers. It is illustrated with color drawings and photographs.

The book begins with an explanation that heat is a form of energy. Every action needs energy, and sometimes this is provided through heat energy. Heat travels as invisible heat rays. As heat enters a substance, its temperature rises. Heat can also move out of a substance causing the temperature to fall.

The section on body heat explains that bodies use heat all the time and that heat provides needed energy. Exercise, such as running, makes the body produce extra heat. Sweat takes heat energy from the body and helps cool the body.

Several sections deal with various ways of heating the home, including using a central heating system, radiators, and convection heaters.

Other sections of the book discuss making fire and why things burn, measuring heat, controlling heat in our homes, safe heat, friction, fireworks, heating with wires, cooking, looking inside a toaster, saving heat, cooking in a microwave, insulating homes, keeping drinks hot, special clothing for special purposes, refrigerators, greenhouses, power from the sun, and finally some interesting facts about heat.

Possible Topics for Further Student Investigation

1. Students might be divided into pairs and asked to use the facts in this book to prepare a math problem for other students in the class to solve. These could be presented as brief story problems. For example, a pair of students might ask: What is the difference between the highest temperature ever recorded at the surface of the earth, 136 degree Fahrenheit in Libya, and the coldest recorded temperature of –190 degrees Fahrenheit in Antarctica? The teacher could collect these problems and combine them into a special math problem sheet to give to the class.

2. In various spots throughout the world, including the United States, there are "hot springs." Some of these areas became famous resorts. People visit these areas and enjoy bathing in these springs. Ask a pair of interested students to research this topic. Where are some of the most famous hot springs in the United States located? Which one is closest to you? What is the temperature of the springs? Do they have special medicinal benefits? What causes hot springs to come to the surface in some areas? Students should report what they learn to the class.

3. Invite an electrician or contractor to come to class and discuss conservation of heat in a home. What is commonly used in your area for the insulation of houses? How is the insulation put in place? Ask your resource person to bring along a thermostat and explain how it works, and how it should be set to provide maximum heating comfort for minimum cost.

How Did We Find Out About Sunshine?

NONFICTION CONNECTIONS

by Isaac Asimov
Illustrated by David Wool
New York: Walker, 1987. 63p.

This is one of a series of How Did We Find Out About books by Isaac Asimov. It has black-and-white illustrations. The book will be enjoyed by readers in grades four and five.

The first chapter explores early recorded history relating to the sun. It briefly discusses the work of some early scientific thinkers. Aristotle, 384–322 B.C., thought that objects in the sky were made up of substances that were not like anything on earth. Galileo, 1564–1642, made a telescope to study the heavens. In 1687, Isaac Newton worked out the mathematics of the law of gravitation.

Chapter 2 explores energy, and discusses the contributions of James Watt, James Prescott Joule, Julius Robert Mayer, and Hermann von Helmholtz. But after all this research, people were still asking, "What makes the Sun shine?"

In chapter 3, studies of the work of Charles Lyell, Charles Darwin, Thomas Young, Joseph von Fraunhofer, Gustav Robert Kirchhoff, and Anders Jonas Angstrom are presented.

In chapters 4 and 5, the reader learns about radioactivity, nuclear reaction, fusion, and the work of Antoine Henri, Pierre Curie, Albert Einstein, and Ernest Rutherford. Many questions about the Sun are answered. Hydrogen fusion makes the Sun shine. But there are still unanswered questions, including what Asimov calls "the mystery of the missing neutrinos."

Possible Topics for Further Student Investigation

1. Asimov briefly mentions many famous scientists. This material might be made into a fascinating bulletin board. Individuals or pairs of students could choose a scientist mentioned in this book, draw or photocopy a picture of the scientist, and do research about the scientist's work. Have students produce a short paper on the computer and post them together with the picture on the bulletin board.

2. Invite two students to study the period of time around 1370 B.C. in Egypt when Ikhnaton was king. They might want to present their story about his belief that the sun was a god to be worshipped, in the form of a scroll. Drawings and information from this period could be placed on a long roll of paper and displayed in the classroom.

3. A group of students might wish to carry out a classroom experiment to show why light is white. One flashlight lens should be covered with three pieces of red cellophane, held in place with a rubber band. Similarly, another flashlight should be covered with green cellophane, and a third flashlight with blue cellophane. In a dark room, prop the flashlights on a book and point them at a sheet of white paper. When turned on, the one covered in red cellophane will make a red light. The one covered in green will produce a green spot, and where the light overlaps, there will be a yellow spot. When you shine the blue light on the yellow spot, the light will be almost white. All of the colors in the spectrum, when mixed together, produce white light.

From *Rainy, Windy, Snowy, Sunny Days.* © 1996. Teacher Ideas Press. (800) 237-6124.

I Can Be a Weather Forecaster

by Claire Martin
Chicago: Children's Press, 1987. 32p.

This picture book is illustrated with color photographs and drawings. It will be enjoyed by primary-grade students. It is a part of a series of books introducing various careers to students. The simple text is presented in large type.

This book points out that at one time or another, everyone is a forecaster. Students check the weather to see if they should wear a jacket to school in the morning and to decide if a family picnic is in danger of being rained out. They make guesses based on such things as sunshine, clouds, and wind.

To get a more accurate forecast, one turns on the radio or television for a weather report. The people who broadcast usually have a good voice and likable personality. Many weather reporters, but not all, are meteorologists.

Meteorologists are weather scientists who study science, mathematics, and particularly the atmosphere surrounding the earth. Many meteorologists work for the National Weather Service, but some companies also have their own meteorologists.

Weather stations and weather satellites gather information which is put together on computers. Then the information is quickly sent to forecasters. Meteorologists use instruments such as thermometers and barometers. They also send instruments called radiosondes into the air attached to balloons to collect data. Forecasts are of interest to all, but are especially important to farmers, sailors, and pilots.

Possible Topics for Further Student Investigation

1   How often is your weather forecaster accurate? Have students make a chart and find out. List dates across the horizontal axis of a sheet of graph paper. On the vertical axis list a range of temperatures. Using a local newspaper, graph in blue the predicted high for each day. Graph in red in the actual high for each day. Over a period of time, how accurate were the predictions? The class might decide that a prediction which came within two degrees of the actual temperature was "accurate." What percentage of the time is your weather forecaster accurate?

2   A pair of students might add to the above project by specializing in barometric pressure. For the same time period used above, they could note the readings on a barometer in the classroom. How did the changes in the barometric pressure correspond with changes in the actual weather shown on your weather chart? Have the two students explain how barometric pressure adds to the accuracy of weather forecasting.

3   The National Weather Service uses special broadcasts to warn people about emergencies such as floods, hurricanes, and tornadoes. Some cities have installed sirens or other warning devices to use in emergencies. Have a pair of students investigate this topic. In your area, are there special warning sirens? Where are they and what do they sound like? What radio station is used in emergencies? Who is responsible for handling emergency weather situations in your area? Have the students report what they learn back to the class.

Let's Celebrate Summer World Festivals

by Rhoda Nottridge

East Sussex, England: Wayland, 1994. 32p.

This picture book is part of a four-book series on festivals connected with seasons of the year that are celebrated throughout the world. It is illustrated with color photographs and will be enjoyed by students in grades two through four.

Because summer is a time of year when it is warm and when the sun rises early in the morning and sets late in the evening, people have time to spend outdoors during this season, having picnics, playing sports, and holding various celebrations.

The book explains that Europeans used to divide the year into two seasons, summer and winter, with summer beginning on May 1 each year. In some places, people still celebrate the beginning of summer on May 1 with a decorated maypole. Morris dancing is popular on May Day to frighten away the evil ghosts of winter.

In China, May Day is celebrated with fireworks. In some places in China there are dragon boat races, which are held in memory of a poet, Chu Yuan, who lived thousands of years ago.

The book explains how the South American Aztecs and Incas worshipped the sun. In Britain, people who celebrated the sun were called Druids. In Japan, Buddhists celebrate O-bon as an important summer festival. It is a time when everyone remembers the dead. The Chinese also have a summer festival to remember the dead. It is called the festival of hungry ghosts.

There are also many summer festivals in different countries to celebrate independence from foreign rulers.

Possible Topics for Further Student Investigation

1 In the United States, Independence Day, held on the Fourth of July is probably the biggest summer holiday. In France, the big summer holiday is Bastille Day. Ask a pair of interested students to prepare a report comparing these two events in as many respects as possible. What caused each one to become a national holiday? The anniversary of what date is being celebrated? What sorts of activities are usually held by people to celebrate these holidays? Have students report what they learn to the class.

2 Many special holidays have been added to the calendar. There are days to honor secretaries and bosses, grandparents, veterans, etc. Ask students to think about existing holidays and then think of some group or some event that is currently not honored. Ask students to write a short persuasive essay in which they promote some new holiday. Have students read their essays and hold a vote to see which holiday your class would support adding to the calendar.

3 The Chinese Summer Dragon Boat Festival is an interesting one. They also use dragons at other times in their festivals, including parades that celebrate Chinese New Year. A dragon is sometimes the villain and sometimes the hero of stories and legends. Have a team of interested students write and illustrate their own picture book about a dragon. When it is complete, ask the students to share it with the class and with another group in the school.

From *Rainy, Windy, Snowy, Sunny Days.* © 1996. Teacher Ideas Press. (800) 237-6124.

📖 *Radiation*

by Mark Pettigrew
New York: Gloucester Press, 1986. 32p.

This is a large-format picture book illustrated with color drawings and photographs that is suitable for students in grades three through five. This book is part of a series, Science Today, which introduces first principles of science.

This book begins with an explanation that radiation occurs naturally in several forms and is not something that is just produced at nuclear power plants. Light, X-rays, radio waves, and the heat from the Sun are all examples of radiation.

Radiation is a way of transferring energy from the source to another place some distance away. Radiation usually travels in straight lines. It can be dangerous, depending on how much energy is transferred. The only type of radiation that humans can see is light.

Just outside the visible spectrum of light is infrared radiation. Some of the energy from the sun reaches us as infrared radiation. Infrared photographs taken from satellites show the temperature of different parts of the landscape.

The Sun also produces some ultraviolet radiation. This can give humans a suntan or sunburn. Ultraviolet rays are invisible to our eyes, but fluorescent substances react to ultraviolet radiation by producing visible light that we see as a glow.

This book goes on to discuss radio waves, X-rays, radioactivity, nuclear absorption, uses of radioactivity, and suggests some projects for readers to try.

Possible Topics for Further Student Investigation

1   Radio waves spread out from a transmitting aerial in all directions. Invite a local amateur radio operator (a ham) to visit your classroom and discuss how he or she operates. What sort of an antennae is used? On what bands does the operator usually receive and transmit? What parts of the country or the world are the ones most frequently contacted? The operator might bring along some of the more interesting QSL cards received and explain how operators write to one another after a contact to confirm it and indicate signal strength, etc.

2   X-rays are commonly used by dentists and doctors to assess the condition of human and animal patients. Invite an X-ray technician to visit your class and discuss how X-rays are taken and used. The technician could explain the dangers from these rays and the sorts of precautions that are taken to protect both the patient and the technician. Perhaps the technician could also bring along some X-rays and point out to students various things that are revealed in the X-ray such as a bone break.

3   There has been considerable publicity about federal efforts and spending to clean up potential radiation hazards at the sites in the United States that once were active nuclear facilities of one kind and another. With the help of a media specialist, invite two interested students to locate newspaper and magazine articles which discuss this clean-up effort. The students should photocopy the more interesting articles and bring these in to share with the class on a bulletin board.

Solar Power

by Margaret Spence
New York: Gloucester Press, 1993. 32p.

This picture book is illustrated with color drawings. It is part of a series of books called World About Us, which introduces young people to problems facing the environment today. It will be enjoyed by readers in grades two through four.

This book begins by pointing out that people have used the sun's energy to heat their homes for thousands of years. Now we are developing new ways to collect and use solar power.

Many houses can be adapted to use the sun's energy. Simple solar collectors called flat plate collectors can be attached to the roof. Sunshine warms the collecting box, and water that is pumped through is warmed up and then can be used for washing and cooking.

Solar ponds, partly filled salty water to which fresh water is added, have sloping sides and a flat bottom that is painted black. Sunlight heats the black surface raising the temperature of the brine, and the heat is trapped because the brine is heavier than the fresh water on top of it. The hot brine is pumped to a boiler and further heated to produce steam to drive a turbine.

A system of mirrors, or heliostats, can be used in two different types of collector systems. Moveable mirrors can power solar furnaces. Solar cells made of silicon layers can convert sunlight into electricity. More uses for solar energy are predicted for the future.

Possible Topics for Further Student Investigation

1. Using a ruler, a protractor, and a pencil on a sunny day, a student can demonstrate how to determine the sun's altitude, or angle of elevation above the horizon. While other students watch, the demonstrator places a box or chair outside and stands a protractor upright on this level surface. Next, the student holds the straight edge of the ruler at the center of the protractor with the other end pointing toward the sun. Then the student holds a pencil vertically so that the shadow of the top of the pencil hits the center of the protractor. Then the student lifts the end of the ruler that points away from the protractor and rests it on top of the pencil. Where the ruler crosses the protractor, you can read the altitude of the sun.

2. The solar furnace that is pictured on pages 14 and 15 looks like something out of a space movie. Have a pair of students, with the help of a media specialist, try to find out more about this largest solar furnace, which is high up in the Pyrenees mountains at Odeillo in France. Have these students share their information with the class.

3. Solar ponds were developed in Israel. One of the largest existing ponds has been built there, near the Dead Sea. Ask some interested students to research this with the help of a media specialist. They might learn when this project was started, how long it took to build, how expensive it was to build, how big it is, how the power is being used, etc. When their research is complete, they should share findings with the class.

From *Rainy, Windy, Snowy, Sunny Days.* © 1996. Teacher Ideas Press. (800) 237-6124.

 ## *The Sun*

by Heather Couper and Nigel Henbest
New York: Franklin Watts, 1986. 32p.

This is a large-format picture book that will be of interest to students in grades three through five. It is illustrated with color drawings and photographs.

The book begins with an important warning—to never look at the sun directly even through dark film or tinted glass. In any unit on studying the sun, the teacher or parent cannot over-emphasize this important safety warning.

This book begins by presenting the sun as our "local star." Facts are provided about the sun and how it, along with other stars, is part of a galaxy called the Milky Way, which is estimated to contain about 100 billion stars.

Day and night, and the earth's rotation make up the second section of the book. This is followed by an explanation that seasons are caused by a tilt in the Earth's axis, resulting in each hemisphere being tipped toward the sun for six months and away for six months.

Other sections of the book explore the makeup of the inside of the sun, sunspots and flares, the sun's atmosphere, an eclipse of the moon, winds from the sun, the solar cycle, birth and death of a star, and the mysteries of the sun.

The last portion gives instructions for making a sundial, projecting an image of the sun, observing a partial eclipse of the sun, and photographing the northern or southern lights—the aurorae.

Possible Topics for Further Student Investigation

1. There may be an astronomical society near you. If students are interested in astronomy but do not know whether or not there is a local club, they could write a letter asking for the address of the closest club to The Astronomical League, c/o the Editor, *Reflector,* 6804 Alvina Road, Rockford, IL 61103. Supplied with information about a local club, one of the club members might be willing to visit the class and discuss the activities of the group and share information about stars.

2. The sun is often featured in pieces of art and in jewelry. Many people have large clay suns that they hang for decoration in their yards and patios. Ask your school's art educator to use art time for some sun projects. From clay, each student might make a sun or moon pendant, approximately two inches in diameter, with a small hole near an edge for threading a leather strip so that the completed pendant can be worn around the neck. If a kiln is available, the pendants could be fired and glazed.

3. There is a stone monument, Stonehenge, in England that hundreds of visitors from all over the world come to visit each year. People hold different opinions about how the monument was erected and its purpose, though most scholars agree that it has something to do with the June solstice. Have a pair of interested students research this topic. If possible, they should secure some photographs of Stonehenge to share with the class.

The Sun, Our Nearest Star

NONFICTION CONNECTIONS

by Franklyn M. Branley
Illustrated by Don Madden
New York: Thomas Y. Crowell, 1988. 32p.

This picture book is part of the Let's-Read-and-Find-Out Science Books. It is illustrated with amusing, full-color drawings and will appeal to primary-grade students.

The author points out that at night, when it is dark, you can see a lot of stars. In the daytime, when it is bright, you can see the sun. The sun is our daytime star and the star that is closest to us.

By using a tiny dot and a large circle, a comparison is made to show the sizes of the earth and the sun. Simple facts and explanations are given to indicate the distance of the earth from the moon and from the sun. The text explains that it takes eight minutes for light to travel from the sun to Earth. From the next closest star, light would take four years to reach us.

The author explains that the sun is made of hot gases, mostly hydrogen. Other materials, such as iron, gold, copper, and tin, are also part of the sun. But they are in gaseous form because of the tremendous heat.

The book explains that even though we are millions of miles away from the sun, it provides us with the heat and light we need for life.

The final section of the book includes a simple botany experiment that students can carry out to show the importance of sunshine to plant growth.

Possible Topics for Further Student Investigation

1. The size of the sun is hard for students to grasp. A bulletin board display may help. Along one edge of the bulletin board, the sun can be indicated by a curved strip of bright orange or yellow construction paper. Information about the diameter of the sun can be listed on the curve of paper. Then the Earth and other planets can be made to scale, and placed on the bulletin board to show their relative positions to one another and to the sun. A few students might undertake this bulletin board project with some adult volunteer help.

2. This might be a good time for some experiments with plants and light. One interesting project would be for the class to raise a bean plant and then to put the potted bean plant inside a closed shoe box with a lid, from which a hole should be cut at one end of the shoe box. The plant should be watered regularly to keep it moist. If the box is placed in a sunny window, the students should be able to see that instead of growing up, the bean plant will tend to grow toward the sunlight. It might even grow out the hole!

3. A picture of a snowy cabin is pictured on page 26 of this book. It has solar panels. If solar heating is used in your area, perhaps you can invite a building contractor to come to school and explain to the class how solar energy can be used to heat a building. The contractor might bring building plans or diagrams to help explain how the heating is accomplished and what the savings might be in terms of money required to heat a house for one year.

Part V

Additional Resources

📖 Additional Fiction Titles 📖

Rainy Days

Blegvad, Lenore. *Rainy Day Kate*. New York: M. K. McElderry Books, 1988. 32p.

Chesworth, Michael. *Rainy Day Dream*. New York: Farrar, Straus & Giroux, 1992. 32p.

Gay, Marie Louise. *Rainy Day Magic*. Niles, IL: Albert Whitman, 1989. 32p.

Gove, Doris. *One Rainy Night*. New York: Atheneum, 1994. 32p.

Mayer, Mercer. *Just a Rainy Day*. Racine, WI: Western, 1990. 24p.

Morris, Ann. *Eleanora Mousie's Gray Day*. New York: Macmillan, 1987. 24p.

Nakabayashi, Ei. *The Rainy Day Puddle*. New York: Random House, 1989. 22p.

Palazzo-Craig, Janet. *Rainy Day Fun*. Mahwah, NJ: Troll, 1988. 31p.

Polacco, Patricia. *Thunder Cake*. New York: Philomel, 1990. 32p.

Radley, Gail, ed. *Rainy Day Rhymes*. Boston: Houghton Mifflin, 1992. 48p.

Rosenberg, Amye. *Rabbit's Rainy Day*. Racine, WI: Western, 1989. 32p.

Waddell, Martin. *Little Obie and the Flood*. Cambridge, MA: Candlewick Press, 1991. 79p.

Windy Days

Amoss, Berthe. *Old Hannibal and the Hurricane*. New York: Hyperion Books for Children, 1991. 30p.

Berger, Fredericka. *The Green Bottle and the Silver Kite*. New York: Greenwillow Books, 1993. 131p.

George, Jean Craighead. *The Moon of the Deer*. New York: HarperCollins, 1992. 48p.

Hoban, Julia. *Amy Loves the Wind*. New York: Harper & Row, 1988. 24p.

Lies, Brian. *Hamlet and the Enormous Chinese Dragon Kite*. Boston: Houghton Mifflin, 1994. 32p.

Lipson, Michael. *How the Wind Plays*. New York: Hyperion Books for Children, 1994. 28p.

Loredo, Betsy. *Storm at the Shore*. New York: Silver Moon Press, 1993. 64p.

MacDonald, Elizabeth. *Mike's Kite*. New York: Orchard, 1990. 26p.

MacDonald, Elizabeth. *The Very Windy Day*. New York: Tambourine Books, 1991. 40p.

Mandelstein, Paul. *The Nightingale and the Wind*. New York: Rizzoli, 1994. 32p.

Miller, Edna. *Patches Finds a New Home*. New York: Simon & Schuster Books for Young Readers, 1988. 32p.

Rydell, Katy. *Wind Says Good Night*. Boston: Houghton Mifflin, 1994. 32p.

Snowy Days

Chapman, Cheryl. *Snow on Snow on Snow*. New York: Dial Books for Young Readers, 1994. 32p.

Esterling, Bill. *Prize in the Snow*. Boston: Little, Brown, 1993. 30p.

Gliori, Debi. *The Snowchild*. New York: Bradbury Press, 1994. 30p.

Houston, James. *Drifting Snow: An Arctic Search*. New York: M. K. McElderry Books, 1992. 150p.

Johnston, Tony. *The Last Snow of Winter*. New York: Tambourine Books, 1993. 32p.

Joseph, Daniel M. *All Dressed Up and Nowhere to Go*. Boston: Houghton Mifflin, 1993. 32p.

Lucas, Barbara M. *Snowed In*. New York: Bradbury, 1993. 32p.

McDonnell, Janet. *Winter: Tracks in the Snow*. Chicago: Children's Press, 1993. 32p.

Shecter, Ben. *When Will the Snow Trees Grow?* New York: Harper Collins, 1993. 32p.

Tregebov, Rhea. *The Big Storm*. New York: Hyperion Books for Children, 1993. 30p.

White, Stephen. *Barney's Wonderful Winter Day*. Allen, TX: Barney, 1994. 30p.

Yee, Patrick. *Winter Rabbit*. New York: Viking, 1993. 25p.

Sunny Days

Butler, Andrea. *Mr. Sun and Mr. Sea: An African Legend*. Glenview, IL: Good Year Books, 1994. 16p.

Derby-Miller, Sally. *The Mouse Who Owned the Sun*. New York: Four Winds Press, 1993. 32p.

Emberly, Michael. *Welcome Back, Sun*. Boston: Little, Brown, 1993. 30p.

Field, Susan. *The Sun, the Moon, and the Silver Baboon*. New York: HarperCollins, 1993. 28p.

Greger, C. Shana. *The Fifth and Final Sun: An Ancient Aztec Myth of the Sun's Origin*. Boston: Houghton Mifflin, 1994. 32p.

Hartman, Wendy. *One Sun Rises: An African Wildlife Counting Book*. New York: Dutton Children's Books, 1994. 28p.

Hoban, Julia. *Amy Loves the Sun*. New York: Harper & Row, 1988. 24p.

Ivory, Lesley Anne. *Cats in the Sun*. New York: Dial Books for Young Readers, 1990. 28p.

Lakin, Pat. *Dad and Me in the Morning*. Morton Grove, IL: A. Whitman, 1994. 30p.

Paul, Ann Whitford. *Shadows Are About*. New York: Scholastic, 1992. 32p.

Ryder, Joanne. *Lizard in the Sun*. New York: Morrow Junior Books, 1990. 32p.

Scamell, Ragnhild. *Rooster Crows*. New York: Tambourine Books, 1994. 28p.

📖 Additional Nonfiction Titles 📖

Rainy Days

Badt, Karin Luisa. *The Mississippi Flood of 1993*. Chicago: Children's Press, 1994. 31p.

Cherkerzian, Diane. *Indoor Sunshine: Great Things to Make and Do on Rainy Days*. Honesdale, PA: Boyds Mills Press, 1993. 32p.

Forte, Imogene. *Rainy Day: Magic for Wonderful Wet Weather*. Nashville, TN: Incentive, 1983. 78p.

Knapp, Brian J. *Flood*. Austin, TX: Steck-Vaughn Library, 1990. 48p.

Lambert, David. *Fires and Floods*. New York: New Discovery Books, 1992. 45p.

Markle, Sandra. *A Rainy Day*. New York: Orchard Books, 1993. 30p.

Rybolt, Thomas R. *Environmental Experiments About Water*. Hillside, NJ: Enslow, 1993. 96p.

Tyson, Peter. *Acid Rain*. New York: Chelsea House, 1992. 127p.

Walker, Paul Robert. *Head for the Hills!: The Amazing True Story of the Johnstown Flood*. New York: Random House, 1993. 96p.

Waterlow, Julia. *Flood*. New York: Thomson Learning, 1993. 32p.

Waters, John Frederick. *Flood!* New York: Crestwood House, 1991. 48p.

Yolen, Jane. *Welcome to the Green House*. New York: G. P. Putnam's Sons, 1993. 32p.

Windy Days

Archer, Jules. *Hurricane!* New York: Crestwood House, 1991. 48p.

Barrett, Norman S. *Hurricanes and Tornadoes.* New York: Franklin Watts, 1989. 32p.

Bellville, Cheryl Walsh. *Flying in a Hot Air Balloon.* Minneapolis, MN: Carolrhoda Books, 1993. 48p.

Bower, Miranda. *Experiment with Weather.* Minneapolis, MN: Lerner, 1994. 32p.

Caldecott, Barry. *Kites.* New York: Franklin Watts, 1990. 48p.

Fine, John Christopher. *Free Spirits in the Sky.* New York: Atheneum, 1994. 32p.

Fox, William Price. *Lunatic Wind: Surviving the Storm of the Century.* Chapel Hill, NC: Algonquin Books, 1992. 197p.

Michael, David. *Making Kites.* New York: Kingfisher Books, 1993. 40p.

Pluckrose, Henry Arthur. *Move It!* New York: Franklin Watts, 1989. 28p.

Robson, Pam. *Air, Wind & Flight.* New York: Gloucester Press, 1992. 32p.

Twist, Clint. *Future Sources.* New York: Gloucester Press, 1992. 32p.

Watson, J. B. *The Hurricane.* New York: Grosset & Dunlap, 1994. 152p.

Snowy Days

Ashton, Steve. *Climbing.* Minneapolis, MN: Lerner, 1992. 48p.

Bonners, Susan. *Hunter in the Snow: The Lynx.* Boston: Little, Brown, 1994. 32p.

Guthrie, Robert W. *Hot Dogging and Snowboarding.* Mankato, MN: Capstone Press, 1992. 48p.

Krementz, Jill. *A Very Young Skier.* New York: Dial Books for Young Readers, 1990. 50p.

Krensky, Stephen. *All About Snow and Ice.* New York: Scholastic, 1989. 32p.

Matthews, Rupert. *Ice Age Animals.* New York: Bookwright Press, 1990. 32p.

Merk, Ann. *Rain, Snow and Ice.* Vero Beach, FL: Rourke, 1994. 24p.

Otfinoski, Steven. *Blizzards.* New York: Twenty-First Century Books, 1994. 64p.

Redlauer, Ruth. *Glacier National Park.* Chicago: Children's Press, 1984. 48p.

Root, Phyllis. *Glacier.* Mankato, MN: Crestwood House, 1988. 48p.

Stonehouse, Bernard. *Snow, Ice and Cold.* New York: New Discovery Books, 1992. 45p.

Washington, Rosemary G. *Cross-Country Skiing Is for Me.* Minneapolis, MN: Lerner, 1982. 47p.

Sunny Days

Catherall, Ed. *Exploring Energy Sources.* Austin, TX: Steck-Vaughn Library, 1991. 48p.

Cherkerzian, Diane. *Outdoor Fun: Great Things to Make and Do on Sunny Days.* Honesdale, PA: Boyds Mills Press, 1993. 32p.

Collinson, Alan. *Renewable Energy.* Austin, TX: Steck-Vaughn Library, 45p. 1991.

Conaway, Judith. *More Science Secrets.* Mahwah, NJ: Troll, 1987. 47p.

Gardner, Robert. *Energy Projects for Young Scientists.* New York: Franklin Watts, 1987. 127p.

Lindbergh, Reeve. *What Is the Sun?* Cambridge, MA: Candlewick Press, 1994. 28p.

Milburn, Constance. *Let's Look at Sunshine.* New York: Bookwright Press, 1987. 32p.

Moore, Patrick. *The Sun and Moon.* Brookfield, CT: Millbrook Press, 1994. 24p.

Palmer, Joy. *Sunshine.* Austin, TX: Raintree Steck-Vaughn, 1993. 32p.

Sims, Lesley. *The Sun and Stars.* Austin, TX: Raintree Steck-Vaughn, 1994. 32p.

Sirvaitis, Karen. *Florida.* Minneapolis, MN: Lerner, 1994. 72p.

Walker, Jane. *Fascinating Facts About the Solar System.* Brookfield, CT: Millbrook Press, 1994. 32p.

Author-Title Index

About the Author

Dr. Phyllis J. Perry has taught in California, New Jersey, and Colorado, from second grade to graduate school. She has been a teacher, a curriculum specialist, a director of talented-and-gifted education, a principal, and a university supervisor of student teachers. Throughout, she has had a strong interest in a multidisciplinary approach to education.

Dr. Perry is the author of 22 books for children and adults, including *A Teacher's Science Companion* (TAB Books/McGraw-Hill, 1994), *Colorado History* (Hi Willow Press, 1994), *The Fiddlehoppers* (Franklin Watts, 1995) and *Getting Started in Science Fairs* (TAB Books/McGraw-Hill, 1995). She also writes plays, poetry, articles, and fiction for a variety of children's magazines.